M Hood

FVL
11.00

# the JOB REVOLU-TION

# the JOB REVOLU-TION

## BY JUDSON GOODING
### an editor of FORTUNE

**WALKER AND COMPANY**
New York

First published in the United States of America in 1972 by the Walker
Publishing Company, Inc.

Published simultaneously in Canada by Fitzhenry & Whiteside, Limited,
Toronto.

ISBN: 0-8027-0383-6

Library of Congress Catalog Card Number: 74-188469

Printed in the United States of America.

To Françoise

# CONTENTS

# *Foreword*

I view the "job revolution" now under way in America in several different ways.

First, it is a human problem. On the basis of the objective studies and the personal experiences related in this book, jobs are increasingly failing to provide a reasonable measure of personal satisfaction for millions of Americans.

Second, it is an economic problem, because the effects of the "revolution" against meaningless jobs are measurable in very tangible economic terms. High absenteeism and quit rates, excessive rework and scrap, deliberate acts of spoilage and vandalism, hostile resistance to supervision and change, and an increased willingness to strike are all symptoms of the problem and they all have a direct impact on plant efficiency.

The net effect is to raise the costs of doing business, to raise prices to consumers, to decrease product safety and quality, to depress the volume of output, and to reduce the competitiveness of U.S. business in the world.

This concerns me deeply. As a citizen, I am concerned about the cost, safety, and reliability of the things my family and I buy and use. Increasingly, it seems that the stamp "Made in USA," once a virtual guarantee of high quality and long life, means less and less.

As a Senator, I am concerned because of the effect of low productivity on our economic vigor and our international competitiveness. Some writers have suggested that changes in American attitudes have so affected our economic system that we will inevitably lose our industrial drive and vitality, that we will become a fat, or "mature," economy, content to suffer a chronically low productivity growth rate.

This is a prescription for becoming a second-rate nation, and I cannot accept it. A high state of competitive economic vitality can be sustained if underlying economic and social factors permit it. We must remember that we are in daily competition with the rest of the world. Many American jobs depend on exports, and our balance of payments depends on the returned profits of American overseas business. But in a larger sense, our place in the world—our ability to sustain a world balance of power in order to assure peace—depends essentially on our economic strength.

In my view, increasing productivity requires both changes of attitudes, and concentrated public and private efforts.

First, the government's attitudes must change, and I am pleased that in very important ways this change has begun. Phase I, and the U.S. balance of payments crisis that motivated it, shocked policymakers into a new awareness of the crucial role of productivity in our nation's economy. In their report on the economy early in 1971, the minority members of the Joint Economic Committee called for a national productivity drive. On August 4, 1971, a group of thirteen Republican Senators, realizing the urgent need for action, called for creation of a statutory National Commission on Productivity.

By September, 1971, as a result of the economic crisis and the economic policy measures taken, the word productivity had assumed entirely new proportions. Once the province mainly of a small group of able technicians in the Bureau of Labor Statistics, productivity improvement became a major concern of policymakers at the highest levels. In November, Congress enacted tax and depreciation measures to spur capital investment, a very important incentive to productivity growth. And, in December, Congress amended the Economic Stabilization Act, which authorizes wage and price controls, to except productivity pay increases from Pay Board restraints, and to create a national productivity policy to be implemented by the National Commission on Productivity. In testimony before the Joint Economic Committee in February, 1972, the Administration's top economic spokesmen, including the Secretary of the Treasury, John Connally, listed increased productivity as one of its four major economic policy goals.

What is clearly needed, and what government must

now aggressively help create, is a national sense of productivity consciousness. A clear awareness of the reasons and the need for increased productivity must be impressed on the public's mind. Government must show how productivity can be increased. It can do this in part by aggressively implementing the Economic Stabilization Act creating regional and local productivity councils. These can inform business and labor of the techniques by which such increases can be obtained. They can help create a new spirit of cooperation between labor and management, which is an essential prerequisite of increased output. It can lead the way as well to promote the adoption of concepts like productivity bargaining and job enrichment.

But productivity is most directly the business of people in production, clerical, and managerial jobs. Government has a motivating, catalytic role, but labor and management together have the real responsibility for change.

What kinds of changes are we talking about? This is the subject of *The Job Revolution*.

Increased productivity is a composite of many things. Increased investment in plant and equipment, high levels of spending for research and development, adequate business profits, good pay for employees—all these are parts of the productivity package. All are well known, measurable, and relatively easily applied.

What is new in the productivity equation is the human emphasis. In this book, Judson Gooding clearly and forcefully spells out the reasons why the new emphasis is necessary. He points out that the labor force is different, that it reflects the rapid changes in Americans' attitudes that have occurred during the last decade. He tells us that the work force is now younger, better educated, more mobile, less highly motivated by money, more interested in personal fulfillment, and thus easily turned off by standard types of industrial, clerical, and even junior management jobs. His findings and conclusions are specially valid because, in addition to research of a scholarly kind, Mr. Gooding spent over a year talking with literally hundreds of people holding blue and white collar and junior management jobs, throughout the country. This direct experience is reflected here, and is one of the most important contributions of this book.

Management and labor organizations, economists, and legislators have tended to resist the obvious fact that the American work force has changed. It is much easier to look at a "worker" as a semi-mechanical part of the productive process who, if he is paid more, will just work harder. A long time ago in his classic film, *Modern Times*, Charlie Chaplin showed us through his comic art why we had to abandon these attitudes. That so many of us still have them is not just surprising—it is a cause for concern and for wonder about our failure to perceive what is so obvious.

Mr. Gooding's great service is that he shows us why we have to change, and he tells us how inventive people and venturesome companies have scrapped old attitudes and adopted innovative ways of reorganizing and enriching jobs. The results, he tells us, have been outstanding. Employes who enjoy their jobs are motivated to do them better; they are producing more and are being paid better. Companies are becoming more efficient and more competitive.

The result of this dual concern for enhancing the participation and satisfaction of the individual in the context of his work life, and for mounting a more vigorous government campaign to motivate productivity increase, is not just a more satisfied work force, and a stronger, healthier economy, though these are certainly worthwhile goals in themselves. To the extent that our nation's output increases in quantity and quality—to the extent that real output grows and the nation becomes richer, the better we can afford all of the badly needed things that must be done for our elderly, our environment, our poor, and our disadvantaged minorities. These are important goals, well worth the special effort required to accomplish them.

SENATOR CHARLES H. PERCY

# *Acknowledgements*

This book grew out of a series of articles on job satisfaction which appeared in *Fortune* magazine in 1970 and 1971. While much of the material is previously unpublished, or is taken from speeches and independent writing, particular thanks are due to my colleagues on *Fortune* who helped bring the series to realization. Louis Banks, who was managing editor of *Fortune* at the time, conceived the idea for the series, and had valuable suggestions about its execution. Sandra Curran, (now Mrs. John D. Nichols, Jr.), who was research associate on each of the articles, brought a blithe spirit and an intensity of effort that contributed importantly to bringing them to life. Richard Armstrong edited them with perceptive skill, and Robert Lubar, who succeeded Louis Banks as managing editor during the period concerned, provided many useful insights. The staff of the publisher's office of *Fortune*, and especially Charles A. Whittingham, the assistant publisher, were generous in their assistance and counsel. Many others, within Time Inc. and outside the company, helped with advice and comments and each of them also has my thanks.

Thanks are due, too, to the many men and women who agreed to discuss their jobs, sometimes for hours on end, and to the administrators, executives and professors who gave abundantly of their time and of their analytic powers in interviews. The reading, interviews, travel, reflection and writing involved in producing the articles and this book continued over almost two years, and in some cases the titles, or employment, and inevitably the ages, of the persons quoted have changed, but for practical reasons ages, titles and employment, as well as other circumstances, have been set down as they were at the time the reporting was done.

J.G.

# the JOB REVOLU-TION

# chapter

# 1

# *The Questioning of Work*

The technological advances of recent decades have brought incredible abundance in material goods and a higher level of education, but they also carried the seeds of revolution—revolution against work itself or, at least, against work on the old, familiar, unquestioning terms.

Awareness of the benefits of technology—new methods of manufacturing, new ways of communication, the increasing number of years that Americans go to school—is inescapable. These changes are visible, tangible, sometimes noisy and dramatic. Harder to perceive, but already having a major impact on the lives lived in America, is the change in attitudes about work, in how people—particularly young people—view their jobs.

The central fact of this change is a fundamentally different perception on the part of workers as to why they

1

work and what they should expect to get out of working. In the past, everyone accepted the necessity of working unquestioningly. If an individual didn't work, he was in danger of not eating—an almost incontrovertible argument in favor of working. Backing up this natural phenomenon were the strictures of organized society. The Bible ordered man to earn his bread by the sweat of his brow. The government—be it king, council, or governor—said man had to work. Everyone worked, except the privileged few who floated through life riding on the backs of others—sometimes literally, in palanquins.

But the constraints and pressures that once made people work more or less uncomplainingly are largely gone. Most people know today that they don't have to work to survive. Similarly, most people know that the old authorities that once ordered the universe—government, church, family, neighborhood values, the boss—no longer have the power they formerly did.

Today's questioning of the obligation to work can be traced to a variety of sources—some obvious, some touching areas of the psyche not fully understood. The obvious reasons start with the simple fact of material abundance. Things that used to be scarce, such as fiber, and protein, and metal, are now readily available in vast quantities, so much so, in fact, that we seem in danger of being engulfed by them. Mobility, once limited and accompanied by considerable danger, is now in oversupply, as evidenced by the countless hundreds of thousands of miles driven aimlessly every year in this country and by the millions of airline seat-miles unused. This means people are free to move as they will.

What has become scarce is time. People find they cannot employ the riches available to them to the extent they desire in the time they have left over from work. As an example, a good deal of the discontent in automobile plants in the early 1970s was over obligatory overtime, surprisingly enough. The workers preferred time off to the extra money the overtime would have brought them.

This change necessarily brings a different attitude toward work. Where the peasant or factory worker once expected to work from early morning until after dark, six days a week, work is now regarded by many as an interruption of the day, coming as it does before the evening's entertainment and between the weekends. The jokes about work breaks interrupting the succession of coffee breaks, lunch breaks, gossip breaks, and rest breaks have become less than amusing in some plants and offices. That work is resented as a bothersome intrusion on what would otherwise be an enjoyable existence holds absolutely for only a minority of workers, of course, but there is some degree of truth in it for almost everyone who works for someone else doing something he does not enjoy doing.

In past centuries and in harsher times, it was possible quite literally to starve to death. The idea of poverty was accepted as a reality of life, unpleasant but inevitable. No more. Because of material abundance, most Americans take for granted a high standard of living—even though it is not enjoyed by everyone—and believe that no one will be allowed to perish. The government is committed, by its own statements and by the will of the people, to assist individuals who cannot provide for themselves.

With food and housing more or less assured for most, and society committed to assisting every individual who needs medical care or becomes unemployed, the old urgency that attended work diminishes. Other values assume greater importance.

But the new values brought into play in evaluating work are also the product of abundance, specifically the abundance of education. An educated, i.e., a technological, society produces more food and materials with fewer man-hours of work than a nontechnological society and that educated society can allow more of its children to spend more time in school. With that higher degree of education comes debrutalization: the unschooled peasant accepted a life that an educated person would find intolerable. The same more abundant education makes men aware of abstractions such as freedom and autonomy, and they increasingly demand control over their destinies.

As the world level of education increased, nations demanded freedom, and this century has been marked by a succession of explosions around the globe—in Africa, in South America, in Europe. Domestically, as the level of education increased, a variety of groups emerged in America to demand the right to run their own lives. The students who rebelled at Berkeley and dozens of other campuses are one example; Indians who demanded their land, blacks who organized such groups as the Black Panthers to assert what they consider their rights, suburban whites who organized to exclude low-cost housing are others. Each of these rebellions diminished the old respect for established, arbitrary authority. The students wanted more say in their curricula and in the making of the rules that governed their lives. The blacks wanted better treatment from society in many ways—in the opportunities available to them, in their position with officials, in their standard of living.

For many of the same reasons, the men and women doing day-to-day jobs in the industrial plants and offices across this country want more say in matters affecting them. They see the abundant economic resources available to improve their lives. They see the struggle against authoritarianism by students and by minority groups. They see priests and bishops arguing against dictates by the pope, and soldiers and officers disputing orders from their superiors. They see cabinet members publicly reproaching the president of the United States. Former Secretary of the Interior Walter Hickel, for example, was really in search of job satisfaction, of rewarding work, when he criticized President Nixon in his famous letter that led to his departure from the cabinet.

The workers cannot help but be influenced by what they see. "Okay," they say, "it's our turn!"

The effects of these challenges to authority are being felt with increasing intensity at every level of business and industry—among blue-collar workers, among white-collar workers and office people, and among junior managers, the young men and women with college educations who are in line for executive jobs.

Talks with hundreds of workers, foremen, and managers in every part of the country for months on end, focusing on what is wrong with jobs, and what should be done to make them better, reveal a striking uniformity about the demands being made at every level. Everyone, whether manual worker or assistant department head,

wants more responsibility. This desire is much more pronounced among the younger people, the ones who are
changing things. They want to be able to make decisions
that are of real importance to the company and its business. In other words, they want to be involved. They
want consideration; they want to be treated as individuals, with their own aspirations, their own prejudices,
their own peculiarities, and their own sometimes remarkable talents. These younger workers want a chance
for advancement. They want to know that there is a
route by which they can move up if they wish to make
the effort.

In general, the younger group of workers is much
more mobile and harder to retain than the older ones.
They have grown up in easy times; they have never
known a depression; they count on the government, or
the company, or *someone* to take care of them. They
think nothing of moving to a different city or a different
state. A job is no longer for life, but is just for as long as
the worker likes it and it satisfies him. They see no need
to stay and take a lot of guff, as they would put it.

Among the blue-collar workers it must be recognized
that there are also a good many who do not want to advance, who are quite happy where they are, with a job
they understand, and "no worries to take home," as they
put it. But they too want to be consulted in decisions
that affect their jobs.

Workers at all levels want to be listened to; they want
their suggestions to be considered thoughtfully. They
want to know what the company is planning, and not to
be informed tardily after all the decisions have been
made.

In short, the incentive to work today is not fear and compulsion as in the past but rather a search for participation and fulfillment. This poses a tremendous challenge for management, for the people who have work that needs to be done.

Beyond the short-range incentive of management to improve jobs for its own self-interest—to retain good people it must involve them in their work and give them responsibility—are broader and deeper reasons, relating to social considerations. This argument antagonizes some businessmen and some managers, who believe improving society is "not their problem." They think, as some economists do, that the sole function of business is to generate profits, and that the rest can take care of itself. Tom Lehrer, the songwriter who often expresses volumes in a few ironical words, satirizes this attitude in his song about the Nazi rocket expert who says: "I get them up; where they come down, that's not my department."

It is in fact *everyone's* department if this country is to remain in sufficiently good social health to provide its citizens with good lives. In this frame of reference, many of the value changes affecting American society generally are highly pertinent to business and industry.

One of the fundamental changes affecting jobs is the diminished familiarity with work. A personnel director of a $1 billion corporation says in discussing employment at his company, "Now it is much harder teaching new employes their jobs, because not only do you have to teach them the job, you have to teach them about work." He was referring to the fact that a generation ago most new employes had worked while growing up, on the farm or at home or in a part-time job in town, but that young people being hired now often have never worked at all. They have to be taught the responsibility of doing a task.

Beyond this, there is the disappearance of the Protestant ethic, the Puritan ethic, or the work ethic. Whatever it is called, it is the belief, once current in this country, that hard work is good in and of itself. Now young people often believe that work is something to be avoided rather than to be performed. The immigrant ethic also has vanished, this being the feeling that any job, however demanding or disagreeable, was a step upward and in any case an improvement over the situation in the old country.

Another factor affecting attitudes toward work is the social ferment churning up the cities, which are our principal workplaces, and the people living in them. (There are many parts of the country that are not yet affected by this turbulence, but smaller towns will feel the effects sooner or later because no one is immune from its basic causes. Corporations moving out of cities in hopes of avoiding some of the problems that they have helped create will inevitably find that they take their problems with them.) The uncompromising demands for more consideration, more accommodation, more security, and more respect by minority groups, and the accompanying demand for a higher standard of living that will compare more realistically with the living standard that America advertises to itself, are responsible for the social ferment of the cities. People want better jobs and better lives and they intend to have them.

There are few experiences more depressing in America today than to go into the houses of really poor people in ghetto areas, whether they are in Oakland, California, or in North Carolina, or in New York City, and see the children, and often adults, huddled around the one bright spot in their lives—the television set. The contrast between the emptiness of their lives and the glittery promises paraded before them on that eternally present, eternally illuminated screen is sad almost beyond description.

This contrast is most striking in the case of ghetto residents, but it is startling too among some of the less privileged white-collar workers, girls and young men making under $100 a week, spending most of their income on rent and food, and unable to indulge in the pleasures and luxuries held up to them as essential elements in the American scheme of things. There is a powerful contrast between what they see and what they can do, and they realize it. It all seems like a cruel and bad joke—on them.

What this means, this barren existence in ghettos and among lower-paid young working people, is that their jobs assume a much greater social, almost familial, importance than they have for people with fuller lives. These workers often have loose family ties, and because so many are transients—newly arrived and probably leaving soon—they often have few long-standing friendships. In this situation, the job has to give the individual more. It is the focus of his existence, and if the job holds no promise or satisfaction, this can mean despair—or explosion.

The different aspects of work and why people do it— why they accept it or why they reject it—seem to reveal themselves in a series of layers like those of an onion. Looking deeply into jobs and the reasons for making work more rewarding, one comes eventually to the fundamental concept of volition—why people doing jobs want or don't want to do them, and how managers get them to do them.

The most important changes are taking place among younger workers, and there is a perceptible parallel between them and the students who have made their wishes known on university campuses. The younger people working in the plants and factories across this country are by no means as independent in their behavior as the college and university students who have created tumult. There are various reasons for this— economic responsibility, family background, and other influences. But these young workers are of the same generation as the students, and they inevitably are affected by the attitudinal changes that affect the students. Their own words, quoted in following chapters, prove this.

All of them, students and young workers—although in different degrees—are asking themselves questions that did not come up in the past. They are asking, Why am I doing this? and, What is my life going to be? They are concerned fundamentally with exploring life and with actively living life, not with going through a set of predetermined motions that lead simply toward death. These questions and aspirations may seem abstract in a discussion about something as basic to life as a job, and few of the young workers would put their thoughts into this sort of existentialist verbal framework, but it is these kinds of considerations that they have in the backs of their minds.

A paradox that colors workers' attitudes is the contradiction between what society sometimes seems to expect of workers, and what workers themselves want. We expect workers to be consumer-hedonists, spending lavishly and buying the lush fruits of our economy, while at the same time we expect them to concentrate above all on their work. This incongruity is defined in Charles Reich's *The Greening of America*. Reich acknowledges the existence of the theory that people are supposed to accept the discipline of their work in order to enjoy the pleasures of consumption, but he says the theory is wrong. "Some have no energy left for enjoyment outside work. Some find the concept contradictory and are unable to resolve the conflict between hedonism and service. Others simply are not psychologically able to go back and forth between self-denial and pleasure." There is no easy or simple answer for this problem, but one way to seek a solution, it would seem, is to try to make work more rewarding.

The reevaluation of work is occurring not only because of changes in attitude but also because the kinds of work people do have altered. Arnold Toynbee, who has spent a good deal of time contemplating these changes, explains what he thinks has brought about this new attitude in America's youth. Toynbee says he believes the hippies and their renunciation of most material things came because work does not seem as meaningful or as real as it once did. The work many people do now, he explains, does not show. They have nothing they can hold up to their children or neighbors and say, "I made this. I grew this. I did this." A father comes home from his distant office with a briefcase containing some papers, perhaps a contract, perhaps a legal brief, or an article, but to his children, it is just a lot of paper. What their father really *does* is beyond them. The farmer who brought in crops, the wheelwright or blacksmith, the clockmaker, they did meaningful tangible work, but the papers in the briefcase signify nothing. If work produces nothing visible and society provides an abundance of comforts so that simple survival does not appear to be a problem, then the question for these logically illogical youths comes out like this, Why work? Thus Toynbee diagnoses the malaise.

Admittedly the problem of invisible work is more prevalent among the children of middle-class families, where the fathers perform more abstract tasks than do industrial employes, but again the example spreads downward as well as upward in this communicative society. Class distinctions apply less than one might think because many industrial and white-collar jobs now seem as bereft of meaningfulness as do the higher-level jobs done by men who carry briefcases. Running a key punch machine or putting wheels on axles all day doesn't give you much of a product you can take home and show your children either.

While the hippies drop out as an indication of their lack of interest in the work offered them by society, there is increasing evidence that those unable to drop out and obliged to work are also suffering from declining morale. This is a complex phenomenon born of the times, which has been considered by industrialists, psychologists, and even government agencies. It includes disinterest in one's work, active repudiation of it, and, derivative from that, hostility toward one's surroundings and one's society. A Department of Labor conference report describes the problem as one involving workers with more education than was customary in the past, "whose occupational achievements do not equal their original aspirations." Translated from governmentalese, this means that their jobs aren't as good as they hoped to get. The result, the report says, is that they "come to look upon their jobs as something which must be performed but not necessarily enjoyed."

The Department of Labor report examines the consequences of this attitude, commenting, "Even more frightening is the possible result of this alienation. There is a potential for violence in these frustrated workers that could erupt in our factories or in our cities. The recent French worker and student riots, as well as our own riot experience, indicate an urgent need for close examination of the sources of alienation to the point of violence." Going beyond this, Erich Fromm, who was consulted by the group that prepared the report, says, "If a bored and angry blue-collar worker on a repetitive job develops traits of violence, anger, sadism, depression, and indifference, he will sometimes be easy prey for demagogues who appeal to his resentment and his desire for revenge." This is something our country, already dangerously divided between rich and poor, black and white, urban and nonurban, can ill afford.

Since the Department of Labor report was published, the situation has continued to worsen. Not long ago Jerome M. Rosow, who was then assistant secretary of labor, produced a special report for the president documenting the continuing decline of blue-collar morale.

This report concentrated on their low self-esteem in the social setting, their concern about relative standing or prestige, and about being looked down upon because of the kind of jobs they do. This says something quite devastating about attitudes toward work: when a man or woman earning a solid hourly wage feels contempt from society because of what he or she does—even though that job is useful and productive—there must be something seriously wrong with the way people think about work and there is an urgent need to change it.

There are still other evidences of declining morale, or of turning off from work, with which the nation is unhappily familiar from following the daily news. There has been a sharp increase in labor dissent, and in refusals by union members to accept union settlements even when the unions' leaders support those settlements.

Union leaders have not so far shown themselves to be particularly alert in exploiting management problems regarding worker attitudes, but this is liable to change as the older generation of union leadership passes and the younger, better-educated union leaders start taking over. These younger men are going into union work as a career, not by accident as did so many of their predecessors. They have studied for their jobs—some have MBAs or comparable advanced degrees—and they are certain to try to get into the act of requiring job improvements for their members. They know that adequate pay and abundant drinking fountains are no longer enough, and when they get a chance they will insist that managements write job enrichment into contracts. This could add a difficult dimension to labor questions. It is trying enough to hammer out agreement on concrete things such as wages, hours, and benefits. The complexities of reaching agreement on intangibles involved in motivational factors and job improvement, while the union membership is looking over the negotiators' shoulders, are frightening to contemplate. It would seem preferable by far to introduce the improvements before they are demanded, at the pace and time chosen by management, rather than being forced to make radical changes, under union pressure, at times not of management's choosing.

The threat of foreign competition seems a more remote argument for job improvement than are union pressures, but it is equally real, if more distant. Already, most electronics production has left the U.S. and been taken over by Japan and to some extent other Asian countries. The business pages of newspapers have carried one story after another about American firms closing domestic electronics divisions and plants—putting thousands out of work—and shifting production to foreign sites where wage rates are lower and worker attentiveness to the task is more reliable. The story on textiles is comparable, and a similar situation is developing fast with cars. Other areas of difficulty include steel, shoes, and bicycles. Job satisfaction has not been central in every one of these problem areas, of course; each case is different, with factors such as labor cost, shipping, markets, and the like involved. But no manager can fail to see that he is in a stronger position to meet foreign competition if his workers are producing at their optimum, contributing ideas for improvements, and involved in their jobs, rather than sullenly going through the motions of production.

Some optimists think the threat of stiffer foreign competition will go away as living standards rise overseas
and wages go up. They expect that problems like those
we see increasing in the U.S.—of worker morale and involvement—will arise and eliminate the foreigners'
competitive advantage. We cannot and should not count
on this, however. Those foreign competitors got where
they are by observing our methods and then improving
on them, and by avoiding our mistakes. Now they are
watching closely to see how jobs can be changed. The
Japanese, particularly close students, are sending wave
after wave of delegations to this country to learn, among
other things, what we're doing wrong and what we're
doing right in job improvement. They will probably figure out how to improve on our techniques in this area,
too, just as they have in so many others. There is no
reason techniques used to improve jobs here won't work
as well—with necessary modifications to suit cultural
differences—in Japan or West Germany. And foreign
managers have the priceless advantage of hindsight, of
profiting by our mistakes.

If the arguments for improving jobs are accepted and
serious steps are taken to make work rewarding, there
can be some startlingly pleasant results beyond improved profits. One enjoyable transformation, which
might come as a surprise to those who have not been exposed to such changes, is the difference in atmosphere in
plants and offices where workers are involved with their
work and feel both responsibility and participation. The
contrast with those plants where they are mere cogs,
driven to produce at a set pace by impersonal bosses, is
so pronounced that it is almost tangible. There are some

factories that one is truly glad to leave after a visit, where the workers are sullen, argue with foremen, claim that universal and invisible ailment, back trouble, and deal through their union stewards instead of the plant people. The plants and offices where workers feel they have a real part to play in the company, on the other hand, are a pleasure to visit. The workers are sometimes so eager to go on talking about their jobs that it is hard to end interviews politely. Those who associate with motivated workers enjoy a far more pleasant, less strained atmosphere, and the absence of tension means less fatigue, better work. More rewarding work.

The choice comes down to moving with the exigencies of the times—not mollycoddling but accommodating the demands of people for more control over their environments—or existing in a grim atmosphere of discontent or active hatred.

If it is allowed to flourish and develop to its fullest, job dissatisfaction can cause expensive personnel and production problems that cost the employing company money every day. Absenteeism, high turnover, poor attention to the job resulting in poor quality, and in extreme cases, willful damage to the products—outright sabotage—can result. Just one example illustrates the point. Pacific Telephone, which along with many other Bell companies is actively exploring job improvement, found that it was losing 62 percent of the service representatives each year from one of its offices. The company also found that it was costing between $3,800 and $4,000 to train each of these hundreds of service representatives. The figures represent a compelling dollar-and-cents argument for improving jobs.

The effects of job hatred on the quality and volume of production are hard to quantify. They can really only be guessed at, but the guesses have to be high. At one Ford assembly plant, the manager said he had to keep 160 repairmen busy fixing defects on brand-new cars just off the assembly line a few feet away, where 840 men labored imperfectly to assemble those same cars. And Ford as a company seems, in general, to try harder to improve jobs than some other auto makers. At one General Motors assembly plant in the eastern part of the U.S., absenteeism was so steep that on "bad" days, Mondays and Fridays, one extra man had to be hired for every ten workers, as standbys to keep the line moving if the "regular" workers did not show up. When the so-called regulars did choose to come to work, the standby men had to be paid at least half a days' wages just for coming to work.

Management that fails to involve workers in their jobs also fails to tap production workers' know-how and misses out on the best and richest single source of money- and time-saving ideas available in the plant. One worker in an electronics plant in Massachusetts expresses it with disarming simplicity. "They really ought to listen to us on how to do the job," he says. "No one knows it like we do—we do it every day, for forty hours every week." The suggestions that workers produce in plants where they feel involved in what is happening sometimes constitute remarkable examples of ingenuity. Listening to such ideas not only helps management save money and improve techniques, it also helps keep the good workers interested in their jobs. This in turn aids in holding on to them during tight labor market times when competition for skilled persons becomes intense.

Just how profound are the changes going on in the way men cause other men to perform is illustrated by the comments of one company officer in describing the people under him. His remarks show that the basic switch in enlightened organizations has been from commanding, from ordering the men to do something, to informing them, to telling them *why* to do it. It is amusing to try to guess what sort of company it might be that he runs as one reads the speaker's words.

He says of the persons under him, "They are thinkers and they want intelligent leadership. If I ran this company like an old-time tyrant, I'd have a bunch of rebels. There are people in the company with more experience than I have, and if they think I'm doing something grossly wrong, I am ready to listen."

It sounds as though he is describing the workers in a plant with forward-looking management and a high degree of worker involvement, but he is not. The company in question is Alpha Company of the First Battalion of the Eighth Cavalry, then on duty in Vietnam. The speaker is their commander, Captain Brian Utermahlen, a graduate of West Point and a man who is trying to cope with the changes youth and the times have brought —and still run a military unit. Utermahlen's comments about leadership appeared in an article in *Life* magazine. He tells how one of his men holding the Bronze Star refused orders to go on a patrol operation. The man said, "It's my life, and I'd like to try to keep it."

This is the big change, whether in a military setting or an industrial one. Young persons want more control over their lives, whether in college, in the military, or in industry or business. "You can't just hand out orders," Captain Utermahlen says, and this is as true now on the factory floor as it is in a Vietnamese jungle—in fact, it is much more so.

The military vignette epitomizes the decline of authoritarianism. But it is important to note that this change in military structure does not necessarily mean permissiveness. It is rather the substitution of another kind of authority: that of fellow workers or fellow soldiers and that of the task itself. It is a profound change.

This revolution of attitudes—for revolution it surely is —is one that is not going to be put down. The best way of meeting it seems to be the approach being taken in enlightened companies, accommodating the new pressures and forces, making the necessary changes so that men and women can have the dignity and the pride in their work that they deserve and that can make that work more satisfying in every way. The army and navy are making sweeping changes in their procedures, loosening up on rules and dress requirements, creating more human environments for the soldiers and sailors serving in them. These changes have been difficult in view of the weight of martial tradition that hampers reform, but farseeing, courageous officers have gone ahead nonetheless. Can the progressive business leaders of American corporations, faced with productivity problems and the stiffest foreign competition ever, do any less?

What is needed, essentially, is a basic revision in managerial attitudes, bringing executives to the realization that a central purpose of every business enterprise must be not only to provide goods and services for the public and a return on investment for the owners, but also to provide good rewarding jobs for the employes. In addition, it is necessary to revise the old attitude that workers are basically lazy and indifferent, and to come to believe in them as individuals who are fundamentally well disposed and who come to work wanting to work. Suspicion of the workers engenders hostility and this in turn produces poor performance, resulting in a perfect example of the hard-worked cliché about self-fulfilling prophecies.

Managements should regard the changes around them at their plants as opportunities, not as threats. They should refrain from following the Chinese proverb about staying with "the devil I know." That old devil is a dangerous one. The situation is somewhat analogous to that which prevailed in the nation's universities, and which came to a head with such startling rapidity because of the volatility of campuses. Students felt compelled to wreck buildings and even rough up deans and officials in order to bring about the reforms they felt were essential. It took all this vehemence and violence to get the attention of campus administrators and to make them understand the depth of the students' discontent.

Workers in industry and offices are not unaware of this method of bringing about change. They are watching—they see what is happening. They are more conservative than students for a variety of reasons, but they may conclude that in order to achieve the changes they feel are due, they too will have to burn and wreck and take over administrative buildings. This could be far more catastrophic than the havoc that prevailed on university campuses in the late 1960s, and there would be a far more concentrated effort to make political capital out of such an eruption. It may sound farfetched, the sort of thing that "can't happen here," but no one thought the colleges and universities would erupt either. No one expected to see the Pentagon besieged, a political convention disrupted, city streets barricaded, or public officials attacked. These are some of the selfish reasons that jobs must be made more rewarding and, in turn, lives made more livable.

# chapter

# 2

# *What's Wrong with Jobs*

The kind of job usually singled out as epitomizing the worst aspects of modern industrial employment is the assembly line job in an automobile plant, partly because the end product made there is so familiar to everyone, and partly because auto plants capture everyone's imagination. In fact, there are plenty of other jobs that are just as bad, just as boring. Some are dirtier, some are noisier, some are smellier. Some, on the other hand, are much cleaner, but provide no more satisfaction than bolting fenders on car bodies all day or all night long.

What bad jobs have in common is an endlessness and an imposed rhythm, a feeling that the job never really had a beginning and will never really end. There is also the feeling that anyone can do the job, so the worker does not have the impression that he is making any kind of unique contribution. Whether the worker is typing stacks of insurance forms, or handling calls at a telephone switchboard, or going over piles of bank loan applications, it is the repetitiousness that fatigues, not the actual energy required to perform the job.

Many employers have not yet understood what is troubling these workers. They go along with the somewhat outmoded belief that by providing steady work and a reasonable amount of pay to their employes, they are doing everything necessary for them. While this view had at least a chance with older workers who have lived through hard times and periods of massive unemployment, it doesn't go over with the younger workers entering the job market in the 1970s. It is among those younger workers, who constitute a fast-increasing proportion of the work force, that the evidences of discontent are the greatest, and it is they who seem least well understood by the older men and women holding supervisory and managerial positions.

Any furtive executive hope that this youth flood has crested is dispelled by figures showing that while in 1965 there were 5.2 million men aged twenty to twenty-four in the labor force, there were 6.6 million in 1970, will be 7.3 million in 1975, and 7.9 million in 1980. At the same time the number of men aged twenty-five to thirty-four will grow from 9.5 million in 1965 to 15.5 million in 1980 —and the older groups, thirty-five to forty-four and forty-five to fifty-four, will remain roughly the same, their proportion becoming smaller.

The largest category of workers in the country today is the group known, in what has become at least sartorially a misnomer, as white-collar workers. The collars themselves range from turtlenecks to button-downs, from long-pointed stripey ones to trim tab collars—they are as different as the different persons wearing them. There is obviously need for a new more inclusive definition, or, as some argue, for abolition of the term. Are white-collar workers persons who do office work but have no authority to direct others or to spend company money? Are they persons with less than college educations who handle paperwork? Is Saul Alinsky right in his insistence that they are simply persons in the middle class with incomes between $12,000 and $18,000, a view with which few others would agree?

They don't know which definition is right either, and questioning them proves it.

What most of them do know is that they are no longer an elite group by any stretch of the imagination. The troubling uncertainty of status they are experiencing is caused by the complex series of changes that is transforming American society and technology. As one result of these changes, white-collar workers—as defined by the U.S. Department of Labor, the whole sweep from professional and managerial through clerical and sales workers—have come to massively outnumber blue-collar workers, by 38 million to 27 million in 1970.

Now, too, they earn less than their less educated one-time inferiors, those same blue-collar workers. Up until 1920, white-collar workers got between 50 percent and 100 percent more pay than blue-collars, but by 1954 they had fallen 2 percent behind production workers, and the pay gap has grown steadily since then. Blue-collars are also well ahead in vacations and fringe benefits, to a considerable extent because of gains unions have made for them. All this is highly disillusioning to the people in the offices, particularly because white-collar work long seemed to be the best way to move up. Compounding that disillusion is their loss of standing. Once they functioned in small offices, often right at the side of the boss, knowing in detail about company operations, while the production workers were off in a shed somewhere. Now blues and whites alike are often removed from the executive area. Little prerogatives such as time off for personal business and wearing street clothes at work, once limited to white-collars, are now shared by some blue-collars.

White-collar workers retain a residual sense of involvement with management, particularly in smaller towns where folks are still folks, because of the memory of those old ties from fifty years ago, but the ties are frayed. As one result, union organizing activity among white-collar workers is increasing. White-collar workers resisted it for years, holding themselves above such organized opposition to their onetime allies in management, but now, that resistance is weakening. Of 752 white-collar unit elections in 1969, the Conference Board (a business research organization) reported there were 422 union victories. The number of unionized white-collar employes increased two and one-half times from 1961 to 1968. Unions are making especially noticeable progress in organizing workers in white-collar government jobs, which were once less vulnerable to organizing attempts because of their prestige and because the government did not recognize such unions officially.

Other problems born of the changes in America compound the angst felt by white-collar workers. Many of them of necessity live in large cities where big companies have their headquarters, and the afflictions that plague those cities implacably plague the residents, white-collars among them. The lack of personal security in their dwellings and in the streets keeps them in a state of fear. The challenge to the status quo generated by youth in universities and in the streets has had its unsettling effect on office life too. Some of the rebellions are trivial, such as men wearing long hair or women wearing pants suits in offices where management resents such practices, but every challenge to authority, no matter how minor, nibbles away at the established order of things, and this makes some insecure people uncomfortable.

On top of this, some who have jobs with nationally known companies and formerly found these jobs a source of intense pride, now find their famous company attacked in the press, maligned in Congress, picketed by angry young people. Younger office workers have mixed emotions in these circumstances. They feel to some extent allied with the dissidents and demonstrators, and in a way hostile to them.

Perhaps the most dramatic of the various transitional pressures damaging the morale of white-collar workers is the increasing evidence that some of them are counted expendable. They are no longer as secure as they were in the past, when white-collar jobs were considered to be permanent. Automation and economic ebbs make them as subject to layoffs as blue-collar workers, in some cases even more so. As office work volume swelled earlier in the century and new machines were invented to do it (the typewriter, the adding machine, the duplicator) the white-collars were the elite of the work force, the desirables, the persons who made the wheels go around. Now, as their work is reduced to fragmented production-line steps, they are often made to feel like mere cogs, and scores, even hundreds, are laid off at a time, as an unprofitable division is closed or a big contract slips away to a competitor. More than twelve thousand persons were cut by member firms of the New York Stock Exchange in 1970 alone, hacking the white-collar nonsales work force of those firms from ninety-five thousand to eighty-three thousand. In the last two years, there have been few weeks that did not see announcements of office force reductions by one or another electronics firm, or airline company, or steel manufacturer, or whatever. The unemployment rate for white-collar workers, which formerly was "usually somewhat more impervious to a general rise in joblessness," according to the Bureau of Labor Statistics, went up more than half a percentage point during the first six months of 1970.

William Gomberg, a professor at the Wharton School of Finance and a former union official, summed up the plight of white-collar workers pungently. "White collars are growing in number," he says, "and they're where administrators look to save money, for places to fire. The prima donna attitude is out. It's the law of supply and demand. Once you're in big supply, you're a bum."

Complaints about white-collar jobs range from the physical aspects to long-range prospects. Airline reservation clerks and telephone operators dislike the restrictions on their mobility. In some cases they cannot leave their desks without notifying the supervisor. They have to use certain set phrases in dealing with customers.

They have to wear headphones throughout the working day in some offices, and they have to respond within a certain number of seconds to incoming calls. They are subject to monitoring of the way they handle calls, without knowing when the supervisor is listening in. None of these practices are universal, but they are examples of the kind of things that irk white-collar workers.

They also dislike the feeling that many white-collar jobs are dead-end jobs. This is particularly true in some government offices, where rigid civil service regulations freeze a worker in a specified spot and make it extremely difficult to move upward. Mrs. Doris Wilkins, a wage-hour assistant in the Department of Labor's Work Place Standards Administration, found that as a clerk-steno or typist she could not move up unless she changed to a "front-office" job. This was difficult because it required learning a new skill, or persuading a supervisor to change her job description. Some supervisors were reluctant to do this, she says, because they want to hold on to good employes.

In her earlier job, she was placed in a typing pool where she had to do a lot of statistical tables. "For three weeks each month that was all we did," she says. "It was very tedious and tiring, doing the same thing all the time. Most pools were like this." Mrs. Wilkins also found that as a government worker, she had a lower rate of pay than her friends in private jobs and she also had less autonomy. "Outside, you feel more like a secretary, you are able to use your initiative, but here they tell you each little thing." One result of the limitations on opportunities, she says, was "a lot of job-hopping to get a higher grade and to get the money they want. Often they don't want to move, it doesn't look good on the record, but they have to." She also thinks that when a worker makes extra efforts, for example doing two persons' work when another job in the office is unfilled, "the girl would like to be recognized, get a letter or something, if she's not going to get promoted." Shifting people from one office to another would also help in some cases, she thinks.

"Young people coming in aren't going to sit around and wait for promotions," she says. "The supervisors are going to lose a lot of people and keep on having vacancies. Younger people now, they have younger ideas, and a younger approach."

An irritant to many white white-collar workers, especially in government jobs, is the apparent preference given minorities in hiring and promotions. Few will come out and say so for quotation, but there is considerable grumbling about blacks "getting away with stuff we couldn't do," getting easier jobs, being required to do less.

The president of Local 12 of the American Federation of Federal Government Employees, John Thurber, whose local's membership is made up of Labor Department employes, says union representation has become more attractive to government workers because their jobs have been depersonalized. "They are forming larger and larger work units," he explains, "and this makes the workers want somehow to be able to be spoken for. This is not possible on an individual basis, so they have to have representatives who can talk to the boss." Thurber says that partly as a result of union activities, there has been some reduction in what he called "intimidation." It has not been eliminated, he says, "but it is much less fashionable. The old Bull of the Woods attitude is pretty well gone."

The workers' principal complaint, Thurber reports, is that "the promotion system is not fair. They call them 'merit promotions,' but instead our people see favoritism and cronyism." He acknowledges that the Civil Service Commission has undertaken to improve the situation and bring about reform. "Under the old system," he says, "the supervisor would choose someone he knew, a fraternity or lodge brother, or someone in his car pool, or a neighbor, and almost always, someone from the same race."

Of the jobs themselves, Thurber says a common complaint is that "the work you do gets worked over by someone else. The first thing you have to learn in government work is to lose any pride of authorship. You have someone over you who ranks you and he can make changes."

Officials of the National Aeronautics and Space Administration found many similar complaints among employes of that agency when they ran a series of surveys of NASA installations to determine what changes should be made. The most common grievances were over promotion policies. A NASA personnel officer says, "The frustration seems to arise not so much from a feeling that the selections made are not good, but that there is a dishonest amount of ritual about the process." There was also much criticism of communication policies. This was especially important at an agency such as NASA, which lives on periodic appropriations and is subject to extinction if Congress so decides. "People at some installations felt they didn't know what was going on," the official says. "They wanted someone at a high level to tell them what is happening, what is planned for the future. This makes them feel informed, and more secure."

Stanley Peterfreund, a management consultant, stresses the need for improved communication in his work with companies seeking to improve workers' motivation. Peterfreund says that having employes who feel they are well informed pays dividends in improved commitment to the company, more productive work, and more satisfaction with pay, promotions, and other working conditions. These factors obtain, he says, at every level of employment, in every type of organization. The better informed the employe, whether he's a professional or a blue-collar worker, the more positive will be his attitudes, compared to other less informed workers. In addition, he emphasizes that improving communication improves the jobs because it helps the workers get the information they need to do the jobs intelligently and effectively. The kinds of things they want to know, Peterfreund says, basing his opinion on numerous studies, are "how my job fits into the big picture, use of products, work in other divisions and departments, the company's plans for the future, the company's organization and financial status." He finds that once communication has been improved, the process feeds on itself, and employes become more interested in the company and seek more information as they learn more about what is happening. One survey showed that in one manufacturing company less than half (47 percent) of the hourly rated employes felt they were well informed on their jobs and what was expected of them, only 16 percent felt they were well informed on what was going on at their locations, and a mere 14 percent felt they were well informed on what was going on in the company in general.

White-collar workers tend to be less vociferous about their discontents than blue collars, out of their tradition of closeness to management, their lingering dedication to the work ethic, and their class feeling that militancy is somehow beneath them. But their discontent is clearly discernible and it is growing. Turnover among them has reached 30 and 40 percent in some cities. Recently, a study by the Paul B. Mulligan cost consulting firm showed that in the average office operation, one additional worker was required for every seven office workers just to fill in for absentees.

Hard statistical evidence of the decline in white-collar morale has been gathered by the Opinion Research Corporation of Princeton, New Jersey, in a continuing series of studies. The research organization charted responses from twenty-five thousand white-collar employes (file clerks, stenos, secretaries, typists) in eighty-five companies over the years since 1955. Taking 1966 as the fulcrum year when the changes began to become striking, the analysis showed that the level of satisfaction with employe benefits was down 6 percent, with job security down 14 percent, and with pay down 17 percent. The organization also reported office employes were less confident of receiving fair treatment by management.

The old feeling of closeness to management, once quite strong, has demonstrably dwindled. The companies studied by Opinion Research were rated by their workers as down 9 percent on keeping employes informed ahead of time on changes affecting their work, and down 15 percent on letting employes say what they think to higher-ups. Opinion Research also found dissatisfaction showed itself in poor performance on the job, more tardiness, and resistance to change in work methods. These hard statistics on the softening of white-collar morale, when added up along with turnover figures and increasing union activity, constitute convincing proof that there is a real problem among these formerly placid office workers. Like other categories of workers, many of the tensions affecting them could be mitigated by giving them more autonomy and involving them in company decisions.

Higher up on the corporate totem pole, and if anything more demanding about what they want and expect from their jobs, are the junior managers who have spent sixteen or more years in school and college preparing themselves for responsibility, and too often find it slow in coming. It may seem surprising that young men and women who can confidently look forward to advancement and important jobs should include among their number some of the loudest complainants about the present system, but on reflection it is understandable. They, after all, are the ones who were in the universities just before, some even during, the revolts that swept campuses across the country. In those revolts the students protested being held down by college officials and, indirectly, by society, and having little or no control over their lives. It was they who so often pointed out the absurdity of requiring eighteen-year-olds to go to war, but denying them the right to vote or enjoy other adult privileges and responsibilities.

Because they have more education and greater expectations, they pose a double set of demands. They want more participation and personal fulfillment, as do their contemporaries in blue-collar and white-collar jobs. But they also insist that the companies employing them work toward realization of the high hopes they acquired at college for improvement of the environment and of society. Their attitudes in this respect are particularly significant, because they are the persons who will be running the companies in fifteen or twenty years. Also, they tend to bring with them to industry some of the antiauthoritarianism they knew on their college campuses. Their attitudes are infectious, reaching down to the stockroom, and up to the boardroom. They are impatient, idealistic. They insist on rapid progress, and a high standard of candor. Some who have looked closely at the business world have decided to stay out of it or drop out of it and seek the fulfillment they desire elsewhere. Those who stay expect a good salary as a matter of course, and rarely show much concern about benefits, partly because they know they'll move before pension time, partly because such long-range defensive thinking is foreign to them and to their image of themselves. (One West Coast personnel agency director, in a curious mixture of baby talk and tough executive jargon, explains "Pension talk is a no-no for the hard chargers.")

What these college-trained young managerial workers do *not* want was explained eloquently by Hugh Spitzer, who had a record of high accomplishment while he was at Yale, but chose not to enter the world of business. After graduation in 1970, he went to work, instead, for the New York Health and Hospitals Corporation, for a modest salary as a junior health program analyst. With his college record, which included one of the top campus jobs—managing editor of the *Yale Daily News*—he could have found a job with a higher salary and the promise of big money in the not-distant future. Instead, he spent much of his time—and he often found himself working late in the evening—trying to improve the access of poor people to health services, a job he found worthwhile and rewarding. "Of all the guys I knew graduating in my class," he explains, "only three went into business. It's happening all over, even to our fathers. People are all asking, 'I'm doing this job for what?' There is an over-all change, but it hits youth first because young people don't have their feet in the past. They're freer to ask these questions.

"I planned to go to Harvard Business School and come out and be a good businessman. Then I got interested in studying business and social change. I decided I really can't go into business. It's not worth my time. What you have to do is put the screws on the whole system, and you have to do it from outside. If you're inside, you're overtaken by the values of the organization. I can say, 'These people are getting screwed,' and if I push hard enough, there will be change.

"I don't want a job figuring out ways of marketing paper plates. This society produces too much, and we ought to stop. This isn't where our priorities ought to be. Kids are frustrated, and are just giving up. They don't have the patience older people do—and that's good. By' dropping out, they make a political gesture, because they remove themselves from the system of production and all that goes with it."

A side benefit Spitzer enjoys in his health agency job is the casual atmosphere of the office. He can dress as he likes, listen to Bach concertos on the radio on his desk if he likes, come and go as he pleases. The atmosphere was even more casual at the office, at the other end of the country, of Philip Freund, who had left a highly paid job as a corporate accountant with Texaco to go to work for a small, youth-oriented magazine based in San Francisco, *Rags*. Freund had gone to work for Texaco because, he says, "It looked like good pay and a good chance for advancement. Those were my goals then. But at Texaco you felt like a small cog. Working there was dehumanizing and the struggle to get to the top didn't seem worth it. They made no effort to encourage your participation. The decisions were made in those rooms with closed doors. You didn't know how you were doing. The company didn't tell you you were important—perhaps because they were afraid you'd want more money."

Freund thought carefully about the life he was leading.

"While I stuck it out, I was playing the game. I had the money and the car and the apartment, all the tinsel, but I felt I wasn't giving anything. Only 2 percent of me was being used.

"The serious error made with me was not giving me a glimpse of the big picture from time to time, so I could go back to my little detail, understanding how it related to the whole. I was just left there. I stuck it out a year and two months, and when I told my boss why I was quitting, he didn't understand. He'd been in it twenty years. He told me he'd gone through it all."

After "dropping out, as they say," moving around a bit, and starting his job at *Rags,* Freund found life brighter. "I made as much as $20,000 a year, before. Now I make much less, much, much less, but I'm happier, and that's all that counts. In any group that gets together to accomplish things, you have a hierarchy, but ours is a horizontal hierarchy. The players own the team. We've humanized the job, so we enjoy it.

"When you look around at opportunities for work, you hunt for a job that is giving back a bit, or at least one that isn't contributing to the insanity. If you can't find one that is giving a little, you start one—that's the generation of the sixties, beginning now to feel its strength. Rock music, home industry, boutiques, they are solid and growing, and the people in them are capable of doing a great deal more.

"Profit is not an evil. The question is, What does the company do with itself and with its profit? At *Rags,* we give people jobs if they can do them, we don't care what their fantasy is, what they wear. We have no hours, we don't care as long as they get it done. I shave once a week. I wear an undershirt to work. It doesn't matter. We're providing jobs, we're doing a service to these people. Everybody wants the same things—happiness, a feeling of belonging, and rewards."

Spitzer and Freund are unusually eloquent, but they are not unusual. Another executive dropout, who had made $20,000 a year but quit to make sand-mold candles and ties, says he left his job because "the company taught us to manipulate people—the aim was to sell at any cost, even if the customer didn't need a machine as big as we were selling him." There are other examples in every commune and inner-city area across the country where dropouts have settled.

The junior managers don't mind hard work, despite what some older executives may believe about the younger generation. However, they accept it with the reservation that the work not be sterile, or pointless, or unnecessarily repetitious. They are perfectly willing to work late or on weekends as long as the work is to some genuine purpose. "I don't mind coming early or staying late," a twenty-four-year-old advertising man says of his job at a New York agency, "but I won't stay late just to write status reports no one reads. I don't like going through the layers and layers of bureaucracy. I don't like the unnecessary paperwork they cause. And I'm not afraid to tell my supervisor I don't have time to do something. I figure I can market myself."

The junior managers are outspoken and eloquent on the subject of what they dislike about their jobs, past and present, as the advertising man's comments make clear. This outspokenness, and the ready willingness to change jobs rather than staying on and suffering in silence, are key qualities that distinguish them from young executives of the past.

Younger people in America have a special, burning dislike for hypocrisy, whether it is detected in their parents, their schools, their politicians, or their employers, and many of the things about their jobs that they resent most can be cataloged under this general heading. They start off by disliking misleading hiring practices—grandiose descriptions of jobs that turn out to be mere clerkships or the promise of stimulating training programs that are in fact dull rituals leading nowhere.

The junior managers also dislike conspicuous display of the trappings of power—the six-button telephones, pompous titles, and thick carpets—if they are only empty tokens. They are quite willing to function in more Spartan surroundings, if they have a real say in decision making. They don't want jobs that involve "just pushing the papers from one side of the desk to the other," as one disgruntled man of twenty-seven describes the lower-level activity at Shell Oil, which he left for a job in advertising. They are sorely irritated by seemingly unnecessary rules covering dress, hair, or beards, and the enforcement of rigid hours where there is no good reason for their being imposed. They resent the feeling they encounter in some companies that the new junior manager has to "put in his time" or "pay his dues" before any authority can be allowed him. Guy Harrell, at twenty-eight, recalls his experience with a major oil company after he completed his studies at the University of Mississippi School of Business Administration. "I was hired by the numbers," he says. "There was a fixed routine, and chances of breaking it were slim indeed. I would have had to go through the whole pattern, which might have taken a thousand years." He left instead, and moved up rapidly at the International City Bank and Trust Company of New Orleans.

Hypocrisy surfaces again in the common failure or refusal of companies to tell the junior managers how they are doing. The failure is often due to inattention or indifference, but many of the young employes affected believe the lack of communication is intentional. John de Pasquale, twenty-nine, executive research division president of MBA Enterprises, Inc., and a former management consultant, says, "The overriding reason companies don't tell people how they are doing is because they are unwilling to make a commitment." They apparently fear such a commitment would require them to increase salaries. As a result, he comments, "Employes feel out in the cold, in the dark. They *need* communication." Deprived of information about their strong areas that should be maintained, and not told of ways to improve their weaknesses, they go into job-hopping, the notorious "lateral arabesques" of business legend.

The ritual moves that dispatch young managers from one city to another at irregular, unpredictable, but always expensive, intervals, are also resented with growing intensity. They seem to waste resources and to uproot people needlessly, costing far more than they usually accomplish. One junior manager simply calls them "asinine." De Pasquale, who has conducted detailed studies of business school graduates of several classes from the 1960s to determine their reasons for staying on jobs or leaving them, says, "More and more executives resist these moves. If forced, they may leave the company. The young now won't accept being pushed around. They don't feel any insecurity, and they believe they don't have to accept these moves as men did in the past."

Another item in the catalog of grievances the outspoken junior managers express against certain companies is the hypocrisy of piously claiming concern for the public welfare when the same company is known to be an ar-

rant pollution offender. This harks back to the concept
of wanting to be able to be proud of one's employer. A
Houston marketing executive for an oil company that
represents itself as meeting its social and environmental
responsibilities says, "I tend to be a little embarrassed
by some of the negative publicity on pollution, on deple-
tion, on industry problems." Many junior managers say
that industry should devote fewer resources to creating a
"good image" in the public relations sense, and instead
take stronger steps to deal substantively with the problems themselves. Judging from currents on the campuses, this will become a more important issue as students now in college graduate and enter business. Dean
Richard H. Holton of the University of California,
Berkeley, School of Business Administration, says,
"Students are strongly concerned about the hypocrisy
of corporate public relations programs which differ
from the actual corporate position."

Some of the most profound antagonisms of junior
managers, which can be so serious they may cause idealistic young persons to leave the companies, are related
to basic company tactics and objectives. These are areas
of discontent still being explored and largely uncharted,
and they often concern company activities or goals that
cannot be changed overnight. But youth's burning im-
patience with imperfection in deed or concept can be expected to strike hard into these sensitive zones.

A foretaste of what corporations can expect from the
young candidates for managerial jobs now coming out of
colleges and business schools is offered by the newsletter
of the recently formed Concerned Business Students.
This is an organization of graduate students at ten of the

leading business schools around the country who are at-
tempting to develop more corporate concern for social
values. Operating as the National Affiliation of Concerned Business Students, they provide a clearinghouse
for information on the corporate responsibility movement, sponsor conferences between businessmen and
students, and run some student research projects. The
director of NACBS, Kirk Hanson, has worked for the
National Alliance of Businessmen developing job opportunities for members of minority groups, and for the
Wells Fargo Bank as a consultant on corporate responsibilities, and is a graduate of Stanford Business School.

The group's opening salvo appeared in its first newsletter published in October 1971. It suggested that investment responsibility might be the issue of the year,
and discussed research by foundations to determine the
influence social considerations should have on investment decisions. The same newsletter advised its readers
that the Concerned Business Students were writing to all
the major corporations in the country asking a series of
questions about their policies and programs. One aim of
the questionnaires was to determine which companies
would allow new employes at least part-time off to work
on social issues.

If it is surprising that young managers with bright
prospects find much to complain about in the jobs that
are offered them, it is even more puzzling that young
engineers are discontented. They have professional
training and—putting aside the transitional employ-

ment problems affecting some types of engineering—promising futures.

But discontented they are, and again some of the same reasons that permeate the entire work continuum in America, from assembly line labor to professional jobs, are evident. Engineers make many of the same complaints about lack of autonomy and lack of authority over the work they do that others express. Beyond this, some of them complain that they are not allowed to give full play to their engineering talents, but instead are limited to drawing board or detail work that does not really require an engineering degree. In their language, they call this "underutilization," and while an observer might suppose that they would find relaxation in doing routine work that does not tax them, most of them dislike it. They feel that in doing such assignments they are wasting their educations, are not earning their pay, and are not keeping up with advances in engineering, which is essential in their fast-changing technological profession.

As individuals, engineers in some firms are subjected to managerial ratings no other professionals undergo. Older men suffer heavy pressure from newer employes, who are less experienced but more familiar with new technology. They have to study nights and weekends to keep up with their specialties, and still they risk becoming obsolete within a few years of graduation. They have little security, and many think their pay is too low, considering the amount of education required for engineering, and in comparison with the wages earned by craftsmen.

Published and private surveys show that as many as 40

percent of engineers would not enter engineering if they were eighteen and had to choose an occupation again. They do not encourage others to go into their profession. They have a somewhat negative self-image; some explain in interviews that engineers are different from other people, less outgoing, less able to meet others easily, more concerned with hard facts, and quite willing to work alone for weeks on end. Their social profile helps explain this modest self-evaluation. Engineers typically come from lower-middle-class families and frequently represent the first generation of their families to attend college. So they are upwardly mobile and quite concerned about conforming. They tend to be less comfortable with abstract and aesthetic concepts than their more broadly cultured contemporaries. This social background may help explain why they are sometimes portrayed, even in cartoons in their own publications, as favoring crew cuts, white socks, and perforated shoes.

The poor self-image of engineers is clearly connected, in what may be a cause-and-effect relationship, with the public's indifference toward them. Engineers are handicapped in any individual efforts to make the nation aware of their contributions because most of them— seven out of eight—are employes of organizations rather than entrepreneurs who control their own time and activities. Their profession is divided into dozens of specialties, and is organized into a state of disorganization by scores of societies and associations run on narrow occupational and geographical bases. Although they are said to be professionals, and want the pride and self-esteem that goes with professional status, they rarely meet their clients face-to-face. Unlike doctors and lawyers, they can't save a prominent patient's life or win a sensational case. As employes, they can't refuse an assignment because it may have harmful environmental effects, the way other professionals can. If their projects function properly, that is no less than is expected; if they fail—if the dam breaks or the new type of aircraft crashes—then the engineer may at last get some attention from the public.

Adding to the image problem is the contemporary abuse of the term *engineer*. From a narrow and prestigious evocation of master designer and builder, it has been degraded to include locomotive drivers, elevator operators, salesmen, even street sweepers and garbage men ("sanitation engineers"). A measure of the nation's apathy toward, and ignorance of, engineers is that television, which devotes whole series to the work of doctors and lawyers and even reporters, has almost never seen fit to give similar attention to engineers.

Industry and government have unintentionally, but effectively, intensified the problems of the engineer in recent years. The system for obtaining government research and development contracts, especially in high-priority high-budget defense work, made it seem advisable for companies to hire complete project engineering staffs just so they could list them and their qualifications, in order to make a bid. The window-dressing engineers then sat around idly for long periods while decisions were reached and the work parceled out. The competition for engineering personnel escalated salaries far out of proportion to the work the men did. Pages of flamboyant ads for engineers filled newspapers. Hiring was sometimes by résumé and number of degrees rather than by real past performance. Supervisors found that the "head count" was more important than salary totals in these crash projects and hired engineers for jobs technicians could do, reasoning that engineers could perform any job that might be required, while technicians were limited. The engineers then marked time or did subprofessional detail work, and became overly specialized.

These conditions, with hundreds of white-shirted men bending over acres of drawing boards, exercising no influence over the projects they worked on, furthered the process that came to be called "deprofessionalization," bringing the engineers closer to the status of factory production workers. They learned just how deprofessionalized they had become later, when defense contracts were cut and thousands were fired.

While contracts were abundant, they could move from job to job, sometimes not missing even a day of work as one project phased out and another began. But the job-hopping cost them a great deal. They lost their pension rights with each job shift. Many went years without even accumulating any vacation time. Loyalty was less to their company than the kind of engineering they did. They couldn't get involved in any community activity because they were eternal transients. They became, in the process, faceless persons filling job descriptions rather than engineers, and as easily replaceable as a worn-out spark plug. They were called the "technology gypsies," or, harsher yet, "the aerobraceros." They had become mass man, with little identity and less status.

This represented a dramatic change from engineering

in the early days of the country. Engineers were the dar-
lings of the nation when it was abuilding. They were
giants, standing astride the land, bridging rivers, dam-
ming lakes, throwing railroad lines across the continent.
They were educated men, and they were few. They
wore black suits and gold watch chains and commanded
the labor of hundreds, or thousands. Then came the
changes, and by the end of the 1960s, they numbered in
the hundreds of thousands—one out of every eighty
working persons was an engineer. Drawn up in serried
ranks at their drawing boards, they seemed more like
ants than giants.

When the economy faltered and defense spending
was cut, engineers finally found out how expendable
they had become. They were fired in droves, just as factory workers were laid off in the past. Some engineers
were stupefied, although it must have been difficult to
avoid seeing the specter ahead. One who understood
what was happening was a thirty-six-year-old California
aerospace engineer, Ronald Taggart, who had been
bounced around repeatedly. "The engineer has no security," he says, "other than being needed at the moment." One reason he gave was that "engineers haven't
been very visible." Now, "they are paying for their in-
visibility." He says a layoff "comes like an enormous
blow. All of a sudden, you have nothing. It's very frightening, terrifying. You wonder what you can do with
your life."

Engineers began to grasp the full dimensions of their
problem in 1970 and 1971. Because of their sudden
surge in numbers, from four hundred thousand in 1950
to more than one million in 1970, coupled with the hard

cutbacks in defense and research, thousands were laid off. There were sixty-five thousand of them out of work in the first quarter of 1971. The figures may not sound shocking in a country used to dealing in the billions and millions, but each of those sixty-five thousand was a human being, a man or woman who had spent years preparing for a career, invested thousands of dollars in an education, and suddenly found him or her self unwanted. No other profession was hit as hard by unemployment during the recession as engineering. If the cold figure fails to convey the full import of what happened, imagine the reaction if three army divisions of soldiers were suddenly and unexpectedly lost. The country would be staggered. But in the case of the engineers, something worse happened: the equivalent of three divisions of irreplaceable, highly trained men was put out of action on the technological front, cast aside, some in mid-career, some apparently forever. The personal tragedy has caused many to leave the profession, a few to leave the country, at least one to take his life. There is a pathetic anomaly in the mass dismissals of trained men in a country that needs its engineers to solve present problems and will need more in years to come as technology becomes more complex.

One result of the mass firings has been a sharp drop in engineering school applications. Enrollments in engineering schools were down by five thousand in 1971 and this, together with the loss of thousands of trained engineers who have changed permanently to other work, means there will be a shortage by 1980, according to the Department of Labor. Malcolm J. Lovell, Jr., assistant secretary of labor for manpower, says in the 1980s there will be seventy thousand to eighty thousand new engineering jobs each year, but only thirty-five thousand new graduates, if the present enrollment rates continue.

The rating system used by some engineering firms in their pursuit of absolute numerical values has also contributed to the decline of the profession, by damaging the engineers' already weakened self-confidence. Professors Gene Dalton and Paul Thompson of the Harvard Business School studied the methods employed by several large technology-oriented firms to evaluate engineers. The companies used ratings spread out evenly over a normal distribution curve, an approach which, by its nature, requires that half the men be shown as below average. (A more humane alternative would be to rate each man against some specific standard; this would mean a lot of bunching up in the upper middle area, but would still allow singling out the superb performers and the do-nothings, both of which could be suitably dealt with, while the men doing well would not be wounded.)

Applying their normal distribution curve method, the firms told the men falling below the middle line that they were below average, which for many of them was a crushing blow. Intensive study of the effects of this approach at one company showed that some of the engineers froze up and performed even less effectively. Others struggled briefly to improve, but the usual result was that their colleagues improved too, so their relative positions were unchanged and they subsided into lethargy or defeatism. The rating system, which was meant to reward and hold the best men and to ease the poor performers out, sometimes did the exact opposite. The highest-rated men, filled with confidence, felt free to move elsewhere, while the low-rated men feared a move and preferred to stay with the company they already knew. In another unfortunate result, older men were sometimes discriminated against by managers who removed some of their performance points and gave them to younger men to "maintain their motivation." Older engineers caught in such situations feel doubly vulnerable because their formal learning has become outmoded and their salaries are comparatively high due to longevity. As some see it, they cost more and produce less. One man sums it up grimly: "This is the only business I know where grey hair is a badge of shame."

Engineers are subject to still another kind of pressure to which few other workers are exposed and which adds to their unhappiness. They are suffering the effects of a new stage of evolution in America, as the nation comes of age. The country has completed exploring its frontiers and developing its infrastructure, activities in which engineers played starring roles. Now it seeks thinkers more than doers, persons who can evaluate the consequences of that development. The public, which demanded more technology, more cars, more electric power, more roads, now finds that it has more than it wants, and turns to berate the men it earlier beseeched to produce them. The car has fouled the air and drained cities of their prosperous residents and of their vitality. Roads have despoiled the countryside with their heavy net of concrete. And the engineers, not the customers, are getting much of the blame. Military and space production are under attack, and cost overruns that stagger average citizens increase the anger expressed toward engineers. Strip mining is ravaging whole districts, lakes are dying, food is suspect. Ahead lie even more frightening phenomena like genetic engineering, the altering of man's hereditary characteristics. Many shudder at the thought of engineers, even biological engineers, stepping in where once only God could tread.

Engineers thus have a special set of discontents, commensurate in intensity with the exacting nature of the work they do. The public has come to look with increasing skepticism at engineering, and engineers themselves have grown disenchanted with the work they do and the conditions under which they do it. They dislike underutilization, working below their level of competence. They are understandably irritated at being blamed for the environmental problems resulting from their work when, as they explain, they only did what was asked of them. The spectacle of mass firings makes them aware of their expendability. They resent being helpless victims of shifts in the economy, national policy, and even of international currents. They are bitter over the country's tendency to credit scientists with America's extraordinary series of space successes when these successes were due to engineering. And there has been an inevitable letdown. As Edward Smullin, a professor of electrical engineering at the Massachusetts Institute of Technology, says, "With the moon landing accomplished, they see no new frontiers," and instead "sense a sort of demobilization" of the vast technological force that made the program a success.

There are common threads running through the fabric of discontent afflicting each of these groups: white-collar workers, junior managers, engineers. All of them want more recognition as individuals, more control over their work and the way they do it, more assurance that there is a potential for advancement if they warrant it. Putting it another way, they want dignity, they want to feel they are in charge of their destinies, that they count as people.

When persons in comparatively prestigious jobs such as engineers and junior managers and white-collar workers are filled with resentment over their work, it is little wonder that blue-collar workers, who long were lowest on the totem pole, have pronounced grievances. They, or at least some of them, are the most angry and most bitter of all. Like other occupational categorizations, there is no clear definition of blue-collar workers. The financial, and social, distinctions between them and white-collar workers have blurred as the economy has turned toward more service jobs and as people who fix things have become more sought after. There are some blue-collar jobs that are genuinely demeaning, others that are physically exhausting. These jobs however are in the minority, even in the blue-collar category, and as they become increasingly difficult to fill, it seems likely that there will be only an irreducible minimum of them in a few years. This category includes jobs such as those in slaughterhouses, foundries, garbage hauling (there are even ways to make garbage collection less disagreeable), and the like. There are also some blue-collar jobs that carry considerable community prestige, such as television and automobile repair, because these services have become so essential—and so expensive. However, one vast group of blue-collar workers whose jobs seem almost immune to improvement as long as technology remains at something like its present level is that made up of automobile workers. There are almost 750,000 hourly paid workers engaged in building cars. They are central to any labor equation because they produce the biggest single dollar volume manufactured product made in America. The trouble is that they have to do it at someone else's pace, in the heat of summer and the cold of winter, subject to layoffs when sales falter and to compulsory overtime when they quicken. Foreign competition can put them out of work for weeks or months, model changes take them off the payroll for varying periods, and new hazards to their income, such as government pollution regulations that may halt production, pose additional threats. They are thus at the mercy of many forces, none of which they can control.

Unskilled workers constitute 75 percent of the labor force in the auto industry, compared to only 10 percent unskilled in all industry, which also helps explain why motivation is especially low.

It is somewhat surprising to learn that in a business as long established as that of building cars, 40 percent of the hourly workers are under thirty-five. These new workers do much to set the tone in the car factories. They bring into the plants with them the new perspectives of youth in America in the 1970s, even though few of them have been exposed to the college campus ferment. Before the 1970 layoffs, 35 percent of the hourly employes at Chrysler were under thirty, 33 percent at General Motors, almost 30 percent at Ford. More than 51 percent of Chrysler's hourly workers had been there less than five years, 41 percent at Ford, 40 percent at GM. These figures for duration of employment are as low as they are partly because of the extremely high turnover figures among a certain segment of the hourly auto workers.

The new workers have had more years in school, if not more of what a purist would call education: blue-collar workers aged between twenty-five and forty-four have on the average completed twelve years of school, compared to ten years for those forty-five to sixty-four. It doesn't sound like much of an increase, but it means a difference of 20 percent. They have correspondingly higher expectations of the jobs they fill and the wages they receive, and for the lives they hope to lead.

Management in the past did not take much time to sound out the workers on what they disliked about their jobs. This indifference was perfectly in keeping with attitudes in an old-line industry that was staffed, in many departments, with veterans who had worked in the business for years and who had risen by their own efforts. Coming from another generation, self-made, tied to production goals and numbers, and not interested in psychological questions as long as the assembly lines moved, they are not in tune with the young dissidents. Many of them feel that the workers are lucky to have their jobs, that they are paid excessively well for what they do, that only a disgruntled minority dislikes the work, and that there are no grounds for any complaint. Managers who feel this way should spend a few days wandering around the taverns and union halls in Pontiac and Dearborn, or among the men at the plants themselves, listening to the workers talk.

The managers would hear expressions of deep unhappiness, and, particularly from younger production workers, hostility to and suspicion of management. A black worker, twenty-two years old, at Ford in Dearborn said he dislikes "the confusion between workers and the supervisor." By "confusion" he meant arguments. He would like to be able to set his own pace: "It's too fast at times." The job is "boring, monotonous," there is "no glory"; he feels he could be "too easily replaced," and that he is "just a number." He would not want to go any faster, he says, "not even for incentive pay."

A repairman in the General Motors assembly plant in Baltimore, twenty-nine years old, says, "Management tries to get more than a man is capable of. It cares only about production." He flatly accuses management of bad faith and lying.

An assembly plant worker at Chrysler, who shows up for work regularly and, at twenty-four, after army service, gets $7,400 a year base pay, says, "I don't like nothin' best about that job. It really ain't much of a job. The bossman is always on our backs to keep busy."

It isn't just the younger workers who are discontent: their attitude spreads in the auto plants as it does in offices and drafting rooms, and their outspokenness is contagious. A painter with twenty-eight years service at Fisher Body says, "The company sees a man as just a tool to use to make the money." Talks with dozens of workers—young, middle-aged, and older—produced few words of praise for management. "Promotion depends on politics in the plant," a Ford trim plant worker says. One of the most damning comments came from an assembler at Cadillac. Speaking about room allowed them for initiative, he says, "They tell you to do the job the way it's wrote, even if you find a better way." A union committeeman who worked on the line twelve years says, "You're tied down, you do the same thing every day, day in, day out, hour after hour. You're like in a jail cell—except they have more time off in prison. You can't stop or get a break to do personal things, get a haircut, get your license plates, make a phone call."

The same point about the need for time for personal business was made by a number of workers in different plants. The complexity of life is increasing as bureaucracy grows. There are more administrative and reporting obligations, more demands on parents from schools, more license and permit requirements, more insurance and medical forms. All this imposes a special burden on persons less well equipped by education and experience to handle it. Some unions provide notary service, process medical claim forms, and fill out income tax reports for the members, but even this takes time and means going to the union hall. Workers on both regular and late shifts find it difficult to get to administrative offices during working hours. Being "tied to the production line," unable even to phone in many cases, often imposes a frustrating hardship, one that blue-collar workers particularly resent because their white-collar fellow employes are not so restricted. One result is that they sometimes take a whole day off to accomplish a simple half-hour chore.

There are other complaints. A prominent, and surprising, one, especially among younger persons, is that too much overtime has been required of workers, who want more free time and want to be able to count on that

time. Overtime diminished or disappeared after the
early 1970 slowdown and layoffs, but workers and union
officials expect it will again become a problem when
demand for cars increases. Douglas Fraser, vice-
president of the United Auto Workers International,
says, "The young workers won't accept the same old
kind of discipline their fathers did. They don't agree
that the corporations have the right to compel them to
work an outrageous number of hours without their con-
sent. They feel this infringes on their individuality, their
freedom. In some cases high absenteeism has been
caused almost exclusively by high overtime. Overtime
should only be with the workers' agreement." Overtime
irks union officials, of course, because it allows managers
to produce more work with the same work force, holding
down union membership.

Other workers, young and old, complain about the
very basics of automobile production: the line, its immutable, inexorable pace, the unrelenting monotony that
never allows a man to so much as get a drink of water,
without first obtaining "relief" from the foreman. Automobile making is paced, in most of its production
operations, by the demands of the assembly line, usually
running at a rate of about fifty-five cars per hour. The
work assignments are calculated, understandably
enough, so that each man's task on the car going past his
station takes most of the time available as the car being
assembled passes him. This means he cannot get ahead
by working extra fast, and then take a few moments or
minutes off.

At some plants, there are sternly detailed work rules
that would make a training sergeant at a Marine boot

camp smile with pleasure. The rules prohibit such offenses as catcalls, horseplay, making preparations to
leave work before the signal sounds, littering, wasting
time, or loitering in toilets. (Doors were placed on
workers' toilets at some GM installations only in 1966,
and only after vigorous union demands for them.)

The foremen, as the most direct link between management and the workers, as the enforcers of work rules
and as the men responsible for achieving production
goals, draw heavy critical fire, most of it from younger
workers. They are accused, variously and sometimes
contradictorily, of too close supervision, of inattention or
indifference, of riding and harassing men, of failing to
show them their jobs adequately. An apprentice diemaker, twenty-two, at Fisher Body, echoes other workers in
other kinds of jobs when he says, "They could let you do
the job your way—you work at it day after day, they
don't." He reports, "We got guys we call pushers who
come around and make sure you're working—they don't
say much, just hang over your shoulder." A General
Motors worker in Baltimore, twenty-nine and black,
says, "The foremen could show more respect for the
workers. A worker appreciates being talked to like a
man, not a dog. When something goes wrong, the foreman takes it out on the workers, who don't have nobody
to take it out on."

The deep dislike of the job is made terribly clear twice
each day when shifts end and the men stampede out the
gates and to the parking lots where they sometimes en-
danger lives in their desperate haste to be gone, as they
roar away in their cars.

The morale of young auto workers was described by

Frank Runnels, the thirty-six-year-old president of UAW Local 22, which represents workers at the Cadillac plant, and which Runnels has headed since 1968. "Every single unskilled young man in that plant," Runnels says quietly, "wants out of there. They just don't like it in there." Runnels, who worked as an assembler for thirteen years and won reelection to his union job by a vote of almost four to one, explained the increased use of alcohol and the growing drug problem as they relate to the assembly line. "This whole younger generation has been taught by their fathers to avoid the production line, to go to college, to escape, and now some of them are trapped. They can't face it: they hate to go in there." Some resort to absenteeism, others to drink and drugs.

Runnels's talk about drink and drugs on the job is not exaggerated. Supervisors find frequent evidence that alcohol and drugs are used, both in the form of empty bottles and discarded drug apparatus in toilets and corners, and in the unsteady gait and glazed eyes of the users. Men in this condition are obviously a hazard to other workers in the midst of heavy moving machinery, and they are generally sent home and are fired for repeat offenses.

The demands of younger workers for change and for those changes to come quickly has caused some degree of estrangement between younger and older workers in certain plants. Generally, the young workers don't accept company fiat as meekly as do their predecessors, who lived through the Depression. This polarization between young and old is seen not only in the production plants but in union affairs. A few years ago, to keep the growing influence of young members down—if only temporarily—UAW rules were changed to allow retired members to vote for directors and officers (but not on strike and work matters). Many of the young workers say they get little help from the union. On the job, there is some tension between young and old. A young apprentice diemaker at Fisher Body says, "The older guys sit back and take it easy, because they got their time in. They razz the kids a little." He dislikes the fact that seniority determines who gets the more desirable shifts. A Baltimore worker denounced older men for catering to the company. "They go out of their way to disagree with the young, they claim the young will be the downfall of the company. Meanwhile they do just what the foremen says and do all they can to follow instructions when the company tries one more speedup."

Some of the older workers are just as bitter. A forty-three-year-old diemaker for Fisher Body is angry at the diminished sense of craftsmanship among the young. "They make me sick," he says contemptuously. He knew a trainee in his third year of apprenticeship, he reports, who "made only $300 a year less than me—and he was a dummy." Another older worker says, "The older men feel the young are cocky, that they better watch themselves. Some of it is kidding, but some is serious too." A thirty-eight-year-old worker on the Cadillac transmission line says flatly, "I resent the younger ones. They feel they should come in and not take turn in seniority—they want the big jobs right away."

Walter Reuther examined youth's antipathy to auto assembly jobs in an educational television network interview a few weeks before his death in 1970. Young workers, he said, want freedom and individuality: they get three or four days' pay and figure "Well, I can live on that, I'm not really interested in these material things anyhow, I'm interested in me, in my ability to grow, to have a sense of fulfillment as a human being." He asked how enthusiastic a young man could get at the prospect of "tightening up bolts every two minutes for eight hours, for thirty years? That doesn't lift the human spirit, doesn't raise your horizons as human beings. This is why there's an absentee problem." Reuther said that in auto production, the worker feels he "is being absorbed by the process, he's not master of his own destiny, *things* are in the saddle, and he's going to run away from it every time he gets a chance."

As attitudes have changed in auto plants, the look of the plants has changed too. There is abundant visual evidence of a new, youthful individuality. A walk through an assembly plant, along the main production line and through the subassembly areas, reveals beards, and shades, long hair here, a peace medallion there, occasionally some beads, above all, young faces, curious eyes. Those eyes have watched carefully as dissent has spread in the nation. They have observed that demonstrations and dissent have usually been rewarded, and that penalties have been relatively rare. They do not seem afraid to take a stand against practices they don't like. They are creatures of their times. Dr. Rensis Likert, a national authority on job attitudes and former director of the University of Michigan's Institute for Social Research, sums up their feelings. "The trend in America generally, in our schools, in our homes, and in our communities, is toward giving the individual greater freedom and initiative. There are fewer direct, unexplained

orders in schools and homes, and youngsters are participating increasingly in decisions which affect them.
These fundamental changes in American society create
expectations among employes as to how they should
be treated."

Much of the blame goes to industry managers who
have done little to make the jobs more rewarding.
John Gardner has a singularly apt comment in his
book, *The Recovery of Confidence,* which applies to
the managerial lethargy that has contributed to the
unhappiness of auto plant workers. "An important
thing to understand about any institution or social system," he writes, "is that it doesn't move until it's
pushed." The auto makers have largely ignored the
worker discontent until recently, when at last they
began to feel the push. Looking at their record over the
years, the Rev. Douglas White, of the Detroit Industrial
Mission labor counseling group, was not impressed.
"They haven't tried to build motivators into the jobs."
White, who himself has had experience as an iron-
worker, says, "The average guy working in a plant is so
turned off by the job, he doesn't think of how it could be
done better or differently. All he thinks of is what he is
going to do after he gets out." The automobile industry
has done less than any other to adopt new technology,
he says, and it has been abetted in this heel-dragging by
union leaders who feared the loss of jobs—and membership strength—that might come with automation.
The industry is basically resistant to innovation, he says,
partly because of its "tremendous commitment to the
internal combustion engine. Rather than looking for innovations, they seek to continue the things they know

best. If you ask them about urban transit, for example, all they can think of is buses. They are in a defensive position, and their response to demand for change is to tighten controls and tinker with the old ways rather than seeking new ones. For years the saying in Detroit has been 'Move the iron!'—and it still prevails.''

Gene Brook, of Wayne State University's Institute of Labor and Industrial Relations, another close observer of auto worker morale, attributes the anger of young auto workers to ''the guy's feeling that he's not part of anything.'' This arises because he is not associated with the product—''in fact a large percentage of the workers never see what they are making''—and because he is made to feel interchangeable. ''This is a reduction of the importance of the individual. It undermines a guy to have someone else come in and take over a job that's supposed to be important in three days or three hours.''

Beyond these specifics, Brook believes the American tendency to ''look down on factory workers'' contributes importantly to their poor morale. ''It is paradoxical that while our whole society is based on factory production, the worker in the factory enjoys the least esteem. Even plumbers, who have more satisfactions and more job freedom, try to conceal their working class status. Hourly workers, whether they're plumbers or auto workers, try to look like middle-class persons, try to live the way they do. Maybe they take a day off every now and then so they can seem to be their own bosses.''

The analogy between campus and factory ferment, mentioned earlier, is invoked by Fred Foulkes, an assistant professor at the Harvard Business School, in discussing what is on the young workers' minds. ''At the universities, there have been demands for pass-fail grades, for more electives, more individual projects and individual attention, less regimentation. Just as the students want to be involved with more participation in deciding on curriculum design, the courses they take, and who should teach them, people want the same kind of involvement in the work situation—more control, more autonomy. They want to be the acting agent rather than being acted upon."

Foulkes, thirty, with experience at New York Telephone and Chrysler, and author of *Creating More Meaningful Work*, says, "Lots of managers don't understand the expectations and problems of new employes, because they are very unlike their own. In the old days, people were willing to work hard and long, knowing it would all turn out right in the end. Those people were willing to endure some situations people today simply won't endure." A special problem in the automobile industry is the discipline of the assembly line. "People *have* to be there," Foulkes points out. "There's no relief until relief time comes around. The whole situation, therefore, is inconsistent with what seems to be going on in society—and it's too costly to change the technology. They don't know how to automate it. So the question remains, How do you make men feel like individuals?"

Stanley Peterfreund, a management consultant, has seen the understanding gap between management and young workers grow in a variety of industries. A serious problem, he says, is that management tends to view young people today as being not only different, but difficult. In several recent major company studies, he reports, "I found that the supervisors are very concerned;

they are coming to management complaining of the different attitude of the young, and asking, How can we get these people to perform? There is a work gap, or a new breed, or a generational gap, no question about it."

A major difference, he says, is that where foremen's orders were normally followed in the past without question, "now the young don't follow orders. They ask questions about what they're doing, and why. And the attitude is spreading up the line, it's reaching older workers. The mailmen and the air controllers wouldn't have thought of striking before, but the example of the young has influenced them. Generally, he says, there is less respect for authority, less loyalty to a particular company or institution. "They're not like their elders, who were glad to get a job and were anxious to hold on to it. Young people now carry their security within themselves, and if they can't do their thing in an environment they like, they won't stay."

Peterfreund believes workers usually come to their jobs intending to work and to do well, a view some of the older automobile executives would vigorously dispute. "If they leave," he says, "it is because the job is not interesting enough. Jobs have been demotivated, so that while the young workers want a sense of self-development and want to contribute, to feel important, instead they are made to feel unimportant. This is debilitating."

# chapter
# 3

# *The Effects of*
# *Job Hatred*

Obviously not everyone at work in the United States, not even all the young people working, feel as put upon as some of the engineers and white-collars and blue-collars and managers who have been quoted. There are still many, probably a majority countrywide, who if questioned would say they do not dislike their work. Singling out malcontents for quotation, as was done in the preceding chapter, is not meant to convey the impression that the whole system is due to collapse, from a burden of rage and frustration, tomorrow. However, it is undeniably true that there are large numbers of individuals in offices and factories who detest the work they have to do each day, and who as a result detest their lives, their superiors, all the circumstances surrounding their existences. The loathing is becoming more widespread, judging both from subjective feelings, and from objective evidence such as surveys. This constitutes a dangerous downward spiral that if not understood and checked can have grave consequences for the nation's social fabric, and for its ability to achieve its various goals. If people hate their work, they don't do it very well, very efficiently, very imaginatively. If workers take less interest in their jobs and participate less in what goes on, offices and plants are deprived of the ingenious ideas they can contribute under the right circumstances. They are the richest source of ideas for increasing productivity that exists, undoubtedly a richer source than the most skilled industrial engineers, because they *sense* how the job can be done more effectively—even if they can't express their ideas perfectly in writing or in mathematical formulas. But those ideas only emerge in the fertile atmosphere that exists where there is a real feeling of participation.

To gauge the importance of the benefits that can come from genuine involvement by workers in their jobs, it is necessary first to examine the unfortunate results of active disinterest. Those effects—shoddy production, high absenteeism and turnover, disorderliness and breakdown of authority, increased use of alcohol and drugs, even outright sabotage in a few extreme cases—have become so serious that some executives, legislators, and agencies have begun to study the situation seeking ways to remedy it.

The most glaringly visible effects of job hatred on the workers have been the increase in absenteeism and in turnover. These are simple solutions to the worker's dilemma: he or she doesn't like the job, so he or she doesn't show up. In a quite different situation, in the politics of East versus West, involving escapees from Communist countries seeking refuge in western nations, this behavior has aptly been called "voting with the feet." The worst jobs, predictably, were those with the highest rates of absenteeism and turnover, so it has been in the automobile industry that the problem first was brought to national attention. Absenteeism doubled over the years between 1960 and 1970 at General Motors and at Ford, with the rate of increase at its highest in the last year of that period. It reached the point where an average of 5 percent of GM's hourly workers were missing from work without explanation every day. On some days, notably Fridays and Mondays, the figure went as high as 10 percent. Tardiness increased too; it sounds like a trivial matter, but where production requires the concerted efforts of all the men on the line, just one late worker can delay the start of the entire process.

General Motors took the initiative in bringing the problem out into the open. Some suspected this was because GM feared it might be the target of a strike if contract negotiations coming up at the time were to fail. One way of preparing positions for such a battle was to establish, on the public record, some of the shortcomings found by management in the performance of its workers.

Apparently following the European military maxim that the best defense is a vigorous attack, General Motors moved on several fronts. The heaviest artillery came from the top brass, the then Chairman James Roche, and President Edward Cole. Roche fired a few rounds to get the range in his 1970 Christmas message to

GM's 794,000 employes, criticizing those who "reject responsibility" and who "fail to respect essential disciplines and authority."

He hit harder in a speech the following February celebrating the fiftieth anniversary of GM's establishment in Saint Louis. While hourly pay was raised 25 percent from 1965 to 1969, he told the Saint Louis listeners and the nation, productivity went up only 9 percent. "As a result, unit labor costs increased by 14 percent." He emphasized that GM had increased its investment per hourly employee from $5,000 in 1950 to $24,000 in 1969. "But tools and technology mean nothing," he said, "if the worker is absent from his job." The company did not seek extra effort beyond a "fair day's work," he explained, but did expect increased output per man-hour from better equipment and methods, and "most importantly, by the cooperation of labor." Roche pointed out that each contract between GM and the UAW since 1950 has formally called for "a cooperative attitude on the part of all parties in improving productivity."

"Here," he said bluntly, "is where management and the public have lately been shortchanged. Here is where we have a right to more than we have been receiving." He cited the absenteeism increase from 2.5 to more than 5 percent over the 1960s, and stressed the domino effects on coworkers, on efficiency, on quality, and on other GM plants with related production. Foreign competition makes the problem more urgent, he said, pointing out that American auto workers get twice as much as those in West Germany, three times more than those in Great Britain, four times as much as those in Japan. Obviously, Americans must be more productive if the cars they build are to be competitive. "Unions and management must strive together to achieve regular attendance, eliminate unnecessary work stoppages, and cooperate in improving quality. . . . we must receive the fair day's work for which we pay the fair day's wage."

Cole took up the attack with a stark remark in a speech to a management group two months later. He said successful operations for GM were "threatened by a combination of people problems. Of major concern are rising levels of absenteeism, employe turnover, labor grievances, work stoppages and loss of pride in the quality of their work by an increasing number of employes."

The problem was thus clearly enunciated. The trouble was that no one really knew what to do about absenteeism, tardiness, and general discontent with the job. It *was* known that the great majority of the hourly workers were faithful in attendance and that chronic absenteeism was concentrated among only 10 to 15 percent of the employes at each plant. Some of those regular irregulars missed one or more days each week. The reasons they gave covered the predictable stumbling blocks of life: car wouldn't start, wife sick, alarm clock didn't go off. Some candidly cited pressing amorous engagements that precluded their appearances at the plant. Absenteeism was notably higher on the less desirable night shifts on which most of the newer and younger employes work, confirming the belief that the problem of job hatred is most severe among younger workers.

Sickness was a common excuse, and doctors' certificates of illness were popular because, when absence is for a proven medical cause, pay is not docked. As a result, there was a thriving market for doctors' prescrip-

tion pads, burglaries of doctors' offices were frequent—
and medical excuses were viewed with skepticism. One
factory personnel man called a doctor to check on an excuse the physician had written, and the doctor, misun-
derstanding the nature of the call, assured the official,
"Sure, send me anyone you got, I'll fix them up for five
bucks apiece."

Inflation has contributed to absenteeism in a back-
handed kind of way, because with rising costs many
workers have felt obliged to put their wives to work or to
take moonlighting jobs. A man whose wife works sees
less of her, particularly if their shifts do not coincide,
and with the increased income, feels able to take a Friday here or a Monday there to spend with his family. A
working wife compounds the absentee problem because
she is not at home or available to handle domestic matters and pay bills, so the husband needs more time off
for these duties. For some, the income from moonlighting jobs has become so essential that, when the main
and secondary jobs conflict and they are forced to
choose, they go to the second job, fearing they may lose
it if they don't, and confident that the auto plant, inured
to absenteeism, won't fire them.

The fullest flowering of absenteeism is quitting, and
quit rates reached expensive levels in auto plants by
1970. The quit rate at Ford was 18 percent in 1969, and
at certain plants the rate reached 25 percent. This did
not mean that one quarter of the work force of those
plants quit during the year, but that there was extremely
high turnover among a small but volatile fraction of the
employes. The turnover figures are somewhat distorted
because during periods of full employment young

workers in their first job at an auto plant will often stay
just a few days before realizing they don't like it and
don't want to continue. When the money shortage becomes acute again, they will go to a different car company, assuming things will not be so bad there, but
again will stay only a short time, and may go on to
repeat the process at still another car company, some
going through three different jobs in two or three
months. This inflates the turnover statistics in a way that
is hard to measure. But the fact remains that in too many
cases workers hate the jobs and won't stay. Managers
report with astonishment that in some instances of extreme antipathy, the workers are so frustrated that they
just walk off the job in mid-shift and don't even come
back to get their pay for what time they have worked.

Looking for the underlying reasons, it is useful to examine the automobile industry as a whole, in comparison with other kinds of manufacturing. The absentee
problem is especially severe at auto plants with their
high concentration of unskilled workers, the unskilled
workers presumably having less control over their work
and less involvement in it than more skilled craftsmen
would. Automobile manufacturing is an old entrenched
industry with old, ultrasimplified methods originally designed not only to avoid waste motion but also to accommodate illiterate immigrant labor or relatively unschooled rural youths. It has a lot of old-line executives
who have worked their way up for thirty and forty years.
These men are used to dealing with engineers and machines, and to thinking in terms of absolutes, not
ephemeral considerations such as motivation and fulfillment. They are inclined, then, to see the problem

simplistically, distrusting social scientists who claim the work is monotonous and lacking in motivating factors. Younger supervisors tend to pattern themselves on the older men they are following and whom they hope to succeed. Earl Bramblett, who in 1970 was GM's vice-president for personnel, said absenteeism occurred not because the jobs were dull, but because of the nation's economic abundance and the high degree of security and many social benefits the industry provided. He cited the gains labor had made, deplored the younger workers' failure to appreciate all they had, and speaking of the hard times of the past, recalled "the way it was when I started here forty-two years ago." Unfortunately, things had become far more complex by 1970.

Further, the automobile industry lacks the relative glamour, the involvement and satisfaction of new-type industrial jobs such as those at Polaroid or Texas Instruments or IBM. It seems fairly certain, from many conversations with them, that given a choice, most young auto workers would prefer jobs in those future-oriented companies.

Another problem of the automobile industry that is no one's fault but that affects the workers deeply is the nature and location of its production plants. With few exceptions, they are in large city areas, tied there by their size, their capital investment, and their labor requirements. They cannot readily disperse in fragmented units to less troubled exurban settings, as many other corporations are doing. The cars eventually have to be put together in one piece, even if some components are built elsewhere, and this eventual assembly requires big areas. Working conditions in the plants, some gloomy and old, do not match those in many other industries. The surroundings can be noisy, dirty, smelly; some jobs require heavy physical exertion, and some, such as grinding and painting, are potentially hazardous to the worker's health. The cyclical and somewhat unpredictable nature of automobile employment is also a difficulty: there were several years of labor shortage and high demand, but suddenly heavy layoffs put 100,000 of the nation's 740,000 auto workers off their jobs for varying lengths of time. The resulting insecurity did not improve the already sagging morale.

In addition to the high absenteeism rates, which seriously reduce production efficiency, there are other evidences of discontent that lend themselves less readily to statistical analysis, but that illustrate dramatically the gravity of the problem. There are more arguments with foremen than in the past. Young workers sometimes refuse to accept orders without long and loud debates— which heighten tension all along the line. At some foremen's stations on the production line, there is a steady stream of sullen-faced uncommunicative complainants demanding relief, asking for slips to go to the medical department, claiming backaches or other invisible medical problems. The foremen spend so much time keeping the work stations manned that they have little time to help individuals with problems or listen to what workers have to say, and their performance as managers is inevitably weakened. They become attendance takers and discipline enforcers rather than supervisors—quite often they even find themselves filling in on line jobs because they have no spare men to fill in vacancies.

Things have become so bad in some plants, order has

been so challenged, that foremen are jostled and cursed. In severe cases where they have had to fire workers, there have even been death threats against them.

Job hatred has serious effects on individuals and their conduct of their lives outside the plant or office as well as in it. Family disruption and the use of drugs to the point of stupefaction are examples of what happens when a worker is totally turned off by his job. Complex emotional problems such as divorce, estrangement, abandonment, and child abuse are caused by combinations of too many factors to allow simplistically attributing them to job discontent. But it seems clear that if a man or woman hates his or her work, he or she is going to be a less agreeable person to live with, and relationships such as marriage or parenthood will suffer.

The extent to which drug use has spread in business was documented in a survey by the Conference Board, which found that of 222 companies surveyed across the country, 117, or 53 percent, reported they had found abuse of some degree among their employes. The *New York Times* reported in June 1971 that drug use in industry had reached serious proportions and was growing. A worker at the Cadillac plant in Detroit told a reporter that his heroin habit cost him $60 a day, and that he was protected from getting caught by the addicts who worked near him and who covered for him when he couldn't keep up. There were twenty-five to thirty of them in his area, he says. Work suffers in many ways: fork lift trucks are driven faster than is safe, and workers have to stay alert to dodge them when they turn and move erratically. One worker described the paint shop: "Guys stand there spraying and think they're doing a great job, but you see the paint running in gobs down the fenders."

The chief of security for General Motors, John J. Ahern, was reported in the *Times* as saying that drugs were responsible for much of the theft of tools, parts, and typewriters, and for some of the muggings in parking lots around the plants. Many, if not most, of the workers whose shift ends at 2 A.M. at the Cadillac plant carry pistols because of fear of muggings by addicts.

The problem is by no means limited to auto plants. The *Times* reported concern about widespread use of drugs in a variety of businesses in centers as far apart as Miami, Boston, and San Diego. In New York several major corporations have had to institute urinalysis tests to screen out drug abusers from among applicants for jobs. One laboratory operator reported that where a year earlier he was only doing thirty urine tests a week, by June 1971 he was running four hundred to five hundred per day. All the evidence indicates that younger employes are responsible for most of the drug abuse in offices and factories, which correlates with the theory that it is they who resent most deeply the inflexible conditions under which much work is performed today.

The effect of all this labor turmoil on the automobile business is higher administration costs, waste of manpower with the constant need for training new workers, less efficiency, a need for more inspections and repairs, more warranty claims, and grievous damage to company reputations as angry customers rage over defects in their glistening, but malfunctioning, new cars. In some plants, worker discontent has reached such a degree that there has been overt sabotage. Screws have been left in brake drums, tool handles welded into fender compartments (to cause mysterious, unfindable, and eternal rattles), paint scratched, and upholstery cut.

The effects of job discontent on white-collar workers are somewhat harder to quantify than they are in an automobile plant, where rates of production, rejects, repairs, and overall productivity are all measurable. There is no simple way to measure the effect on a bank's customers when clerks are rude, or when telephone calls go unanswered, or when frequent billing errors appear on statements. Personnel turnover is one gauge, an important one, but one not necessarily related to the efficiency with which the jobs are done. Measurable or not, depersonalization has had its effects on many white-collar jobs and has caused increased turnover, more errors, and lower performance. Depersonalization has also diminished the already-weakened feeling of alliance between white-collar workers and management. This feeling was strong when clerks were few and were almost considered as part of management, working the same hours, wearing the same clothes, doing clean office work instead of factory labor. Now, however, a girl at one of thirty desks in a room, processing insurance forms all day, from starting to quitting time, or running a key punch machine, doesn't feel particularly close to the executives running the company. As a result, the old feeling of involvement with management has disappeared in some offices. A twenty-eight-year-old bank worker, asked about her feeling toward her employer, says, "Loyalty? That is archaic. The question is whether you like the job, what you need and want. The job is not loyal to you." Another bank worker says simply, "You work for your money. Nothing is given to you."

The company with perhaps the most pressing interest in avoiding white-collar discontent in the United States is the American Telephone and Telegraph Company, which through its subsidiary companies, has 772,000 employes and is the largest employer in the nation. Most of its workers are in the white-collar category, and for that matter, many who are technically rated as blue-collar, such as repairmen, have jobs that could be held to be of white-collar status. AT&T's Pacific Telephone found that turnover among operators in the Los Angeles central area reached 64.6 percent in 1969. This meant that the traffic division, in which operators work, had to recruit, hire, and train 1,699 new operators, at a cost of $1 million, money that could otherwise have been used more profitably. Vigorous efforts and ingenious experiments intended to improve white-collar jobs are being pursued, as will be discussed in a later chapter. The vast majority of such jobs, however, such as airline reservation clerk, bank teller, insurance office worker, government worker, are at best standing still in satisfaction and status, if not deteriorating. As a result, restless workers are seeking ways of helping themselves, because they feel management is not helping them. An obvious recourse many turn to is unionism. The traditional reluctance among white-collar workers to associate themselves with what some status-concerned clerks thought of as lower-class militancy has been diminishing for several years. Howard Coughlin, president of the eighty thousand-member Office and Professional Employes International Union, says, "Those who have felt that unionism may cost them something in the way of loss of dignity are slowly but surely acquiring a change of viewpoint." He cites the changes in white-collar jobs that automation has brought, altering the work setting from an office to a factory atmosphere. Another factor making white-collar workers more receptive to union efforts is the example of professional workers such as teachers and airline pilots, who willingly trade the "status" of nonunionism for the benefits collective bargaining brings them.

Unions are applying a variety of pressures in their attempts to organize the increasingly willing white-collar workers. They have taken close aim, for example, on the 850,000 bank workers they estimate are eligible for union membership. Citing the lower average pay of bank employes (which the OPEIU calculated as $2.68 hourly in 1969, compared to $3.34 average for all workers in manufacturing and durable goods) and the size of union banking business (annual deposits of $3 billion, pension funds of between $20 and $35 billion under union influence, and cash flow for union-involved welfare funds between $8 and $14 billion annually), they reckon that banks wanting union funds should accept being organized as a form of "dues."

The white-collar force may well be headed toward a much greater degree of union organization, if pressed hard enough by circumstances and if not given relief by imaginative managers. Jerry Wurf, international president of the American Federation of State, County, and Municipal Employes, the fastest-growing public employes union in the country, predicts, understandably, that the trend toward white-collar unionization will intensify. He observes that there is less distinction between classes in the U.S. now than in the past. "White-collar America is faced with more and more pressures, with technical changes and computers offering different kinds of opportunities, and with the breakthrough of minority groups whose expectations are rising faster than their ability to keep up with them." He believes the real impetus to change white-collar jobs will come from the young workers, who are not concerned about leaving a job, who do not remember the Depression, who are far less constrained about demanding raises and improved job conditions.

Dr. Eric Trist, of the Wharton School of Finance, one of America's ranking philosophers on socio-technical systems, says, "The white-collar workers have been the most neglected group in the United States. The skilled blue-collar worker has got it made. He is a professional and he does unprogrammed work. He is getting more and more money and working less and less hours. The white-collar workers have been rather docile. They haven't had the clout through unionization to keep up with inflation."

It is the comparisons they continually make, consciously and unconsciously, between their status and living standards and those of other groups that are so galling to white-collar workers. As Dr. Trist explains, the blue-collars have moved ahead on several fronts, and white-collars have fallen back, relatively if not absolutely. Once they had it made; they were at the top of the heap among nonexecutives. Now, as they become more aware of the erosion of their status and of their increasing dispensability, and as their work becomes more dehumanized, managements will have to move quickly and skillfully if they are to head off the unions in the contest for white-collar leadership.

The response of junior managers to unsatisfactory job conditions can be briefly described. If they don't like the job or the company, they leave. At least, that was the common pattern during recent years when jobs were readily available. More privileged economically, often with fewer family responsibilities and expenses, and with more easily marketable abilities to sell, they can still take this course with relative assurance of finding other work. Part of the job shifts among junior managers are exploratory and don't necessarily indicate dissatisfaction, of course. Few young people now intend to stay indefinitely in their first job. The first job, in fact, is considered as an extension of college training by many. They want to see what it's like to work; they may want to check out the industry to see if it interests them just as they would check out a college course by auditing a few lectures. They may take a job because it's in a part of the country that intrigues them. Whatever the reasons, and despite the economic slump of 1970 and 1971, they continue to seek change. Most companies still expect to lose roughly half their newly hired college graduates in the first three to five years, with some of those who leave going into public service, some changing companies, some going back to school, others just dropping out.

The junior managers don't intentionally make mistakes or sabotage production—they usually aren't the type for these approaches—and they rarely fake sickness to stay home and collect their pay, but by quitting they cost their employers thousands of dollars each for recruiting and training and replacing. They also damage the company's reputation by leaving, marking it as a place at which people do not want to stay. Word of this sort gets around rapidly on the youth grapevine. Although leaving a job seems like a rather passive tactic, it actually is a very damning one at the junior manager level, somewhat akin to breaking an engagement. The junior manager has usually been selected from among many candidates, and management has counted on him to grow, contribute ideas and energy to the company, and eventually to move into an important job. When he leaves, that potential, and the investment made in him, is all lost.

Throughout the whole gamut of workers, from production line to professionals, from white-collar to managerial levels, the most significant loss to managers where there is low participation and poor motivation is that of the human contributions they can make. The flow of ideas that comes from workers who are really interested and involved in their tasks can be remarkable. The feeling of cooperation, of working on a common task in which each person plays his part, is also invaluable. It makes a day at work a comparative pleasure, instead of an eight-hour hassle, as some of these younger workers would term it. So, almost as important as the turnover reduction and better quality that accompany improvement of jobs is an improvement of the atmosphere in which everyone works. This includes the managers too. Where jobs are bad, they are worn down every day by the conflicting demands of the superior executives above them, insisting on high performance, and the reluctance of the workers below them to meet those standards, those goals. They are truly the men in the middle, under pressure and under scrutiny from above and from below. When jobs are improved and people contribute willingly rather than reluctantly, when they volunteer ideas rather than just seeking to get out of the plant or office as early as possible, that is when the job of the manager begins to become rewarding—even inspiring.

# chapter
# 4

# *Alleviate, Mitigate, Palliate*

It is an impressive collection of problems that managers face in dealing with employe discontent. In fact, it is a somewhat intimidating collection. Some of the problems have been around a long time and have just become worse lately; others have emerged fairly recently. Because some are historic and others brand-new, attempts at solving or resolving them are at different stages. But one thing seems quite clear: there are palliatives that may ease the severity or mask the importance of the problems, but don't solve them, and there are long-range thorough-going revisions of procedures and attitudes that have a good chance of providing permanent solutions.

One basic and obvious tactic for lowering the complaint level is to increase pay. Some managements have tended to assume, from force of habit and from the pattern of the past, that good pay and fringe benefits are enough to command worker loyalty and performance. This used to be true, when a job was for survival and the fifty-four-hour week was considered normal. A raise meant a higher standard of living, and it meant the company cared about you. Now, salary or wage raises have less impact, at least they do among those who are basically discontent with their work. General Motors provided wage raises every year except one from 1960 to 1970 for hourly workers, and watched absenteeism increase over the same period from around 2.5 percent to more than 5 percent, while complaints about defective work increased and the number of labor grievances mounted. The pay increases had less impact because of the now taken-for-granted expectation of a richer standard of living each year, as a matter of course. Their impact was diminished too by inflation. In addition, they made little impression on the workers as marks of company esteem because the employes knew that workers were sought after and in short supply, so the company had little choice in a competitive labor market but to raise wages. On top of that, they knew management had been forced to give raises by union pressures, rather than giving them freely as a mark of appreciation.

General Motors still presents money as a powerful motivator; it tells its workers that even the lowest-paid hourly GM employes are in the top one-third of the U.S. income spectrum. But many learned theoreticians disagree with the automobile executives about money as a reward, arguing that men work for more than pay and that their other psychological needs must be satisfied.

The men bear the experts out, refusing by the dozens and the scores to come in to work or, once there, refusing to stay.

The impact of pay raises is lessened too by the fact that many workers either have working wives or moonlight jobs, which means that their factory salary is not as crucial to their finances as it would have been in the past. When workers say, "You couldn't pay me enough to do that job," they literally mean it. Money is not the inducer, or the soother, that it once was.

Some will deny that this change has occurred, or that it has any real importance. Denials will come with particular vehemence from labor union officials, whose principal stock in trade is the obtention of wage increases at each contract negotiation. And some individual workers will assert that money is the most important thing in their lives and that more money is therefore of primordial importance. But many of them want other values as well. In interviewing dozens of blue-collar and white-collar workers, it became clear that for many the money was adequate, but that other aspects of the jobs were highly irritating.

A companion attempt to reduce worker discontent that complements higher pay is shorter hours. This can take the form of a shorter workday, a shorter week, longer vacations, or periodic leaves. There are some who find this approach at least a partial solution. But when one examines the concept closely, it is evident that it is just another way of temporizing. It is as though management admits, "Okay, this is a lousy job and you hate doing it so instead of trying to find ways to make jobs better, we're just going to shorten the time you have to do it each day."

The four-day week, currently enjoying a certain vogue, is in many cases an expression of this managerial philosophy. You have four days of misery instead of five. And in many cases where it is being used, it has definite advantages for management, offering important savings of one sort or another. Compressing work weeks into four or even three long days and alternating those working days, for example, can permit 24-hour-per-day use of expensive computer equipment that would otherwise be idle 128 hours a week. Some workers find the long "weekends" allowed them under four-day-week arrangements enjoyable or convenient, but there are also some who do not like the arrangement, who dislike periodic rotation of their work week and the effects this has on their sleeping and eating habits, their recreation, their family lives.

Chrysler and the UAW have studied the implications of the four-day week for almost a year, and have reached an agreement, for the present, to disagree. Chrysler, and other automobile manufacturers, hold that the four-day week would create severe problems in building cars. They fear a day ten hours long would cause productivity to decline. The ten-hour day would also preclude running a third shift, so there might be a net loss in production, and plant productivity, rather than a gain. Douglas Fraser, UAW vice-president, has pressed Chrysler to begin an experiment, and there is considerable—although not unanimous—support for the scheme among the members, some of whom wear jackets and shirts emblazoned with the four-day-week legend in the plants.

Longer vacations, another of the palliative approaches, also cut down on the time the employe has to spend working, and they have the additional advantage of allowing a fresh view of the job after an absence. Vacations normally are lengthened as the years of company service increase, and because there is less absenteeism among employes with longer service, it could be argued from the evidence that longer vacations are a positive factor in improving morale. This is no doubt true in many cases; the employe with four weeks' vacation gets a real rest, and he or she has the comforting knowledge that the company is expressing esteem for him or her by awarding a long period off from work. But even this recognition is in a sense begging the question, because it has no effect on the nature or satisfaction of the job itself—it is merely a lengthened surcease from something that, if relief from it is so important, must be assumed to be pretty awful. Again, union leaders push for longer vacations, because they represent tangible gains they can point to and quantify, and because the more workers there are on vacation, the more jobs there will be, and the greater will be union membership and dues. Union pressure for earlier retirement falls into this same category: end the misery, get the man out of the plant and onto his back porch, at fifty-five rather than sixty.

An old-fashioned way of coping with worker discontent that is still used, and still has certain advantages, is that of providing more creature comforts. This approach can range from basics such as better washrooms and drinking fountains to subsidized cafeterias, company-paid parking, and other types of creature comforts. No one, obviously, is going to object to being pampered in these ways. They have their uses. But most workers, even at the blue-collar industrial level, are fully accustomed to certain basic comforts and do not consider such blandishments as extraordinary, or as anything for which they should be particularly grateful. A city newspaper that ran an excellent employe cafeteria with food at subsidized prices rarely won praise for the facility, but received numerous complaints about the food and menu choices. Some workers, particularly those cynics from the editorial staff of the paper, criticized management for operating the cafeteria, holding that it was done so that reporters and editors would eat on the premises rather than going out and could be summoned over the loudspeaker system to deal with urgent news stories. Such is the gratitude these efforts are liable to win.

The limited impact creature comforts have on employes bears out the findings of the late Abraham H. Maslow, who established a hierarchical order of satisfaction to evaluate men's motivation levels. The basics, Maslow said, are physiological needs such as food and shelter. Once this level of requirements is satisfied, the priority then escalates to security and safety, then to belonging, then to ego satisfaction and esteem, culminating with self-actualization—man's exploration and realization of his ultimate capabilities. With the fundamentals taken care of—food, shelter, and a degree of security all assured—the more spiritual concerns begin to have real importance. The man then insists on being his own man, on having some dignity, some authority over his work, some real responsibility for it.

# chapter
# 5

# *How the Job Revolution Changes Jobs*

Looking out over the long-range, it is evident to many enlightened executives that the factors that have made job discontent a worrisome problem in business are going to intensify, and that means must be found to cope with them. The tendency of government to assure economic survival to all citizens is certainly not going to diminish in the foreseeable future; proposals such as the guaranteed income will strengthen it if anything. Similarly, the desire for more self-determination, now most evident among younger workers, and better-educated workers, is not going to go away. As more students enter the job market, with more education, and more exposure to the new academic freedoms and the new relationships between students and teachers, and between parents and children, they are going to demand more say about their lives in the offices and plants where they work. This applies up and down the line, from managerial trainees to engineers to production line workers. So, the problem is not going to subside, and will more probably intensify.

The way to approach it, then, may be to stop regarding it as a problem and to consider it an opportunity. If these newly independent, demanding, better educated workers can be made to feel involved in their work, better work will be done, at less cost, with fewer errors, in a more pleasant atmosphere. This is the approach that is being taken by executives in a broad variety of plants and offices, and the results have been striking. Not every new technique or every theoretical idea works when put into application. Some of the executives who anticipated the need for change and dared to explore unfamiliar territory sometimes found themselves on paths that proved to lead nowhere, or even led into trouble. Fresh routes had to be hacked arduously through administrative undergrowth, many of them only to be abandoned, at high cost in energy and treasure. But some of the investigations have been rewarding in the extreme, and have led to higher production, better quality, greater profits, and lower turnover and absenteeism. The other kind of reward, less tangible but equally important in human terms to concerned managements, has been the change in climate in plants where the outlook on work has been altered. No one pretends that in even the most enlightened factory or office the situation has become idyllic, that work has become play. But in some plants there is now a discernible mutuality of interest between management and the working force that results in a warmer atmosphere, an air of trust, so that workers who in the past might have spoken sullenly about what "they" want, now talk enthusiastically about what "we" are doing.

The by-product benefits of better working environments, with less tension, better morale, fewer disputes and grievances, are also enjoyed by the managers and executives of such enterprises, so there are personal as well as productivity rewards at all levels of the enterprise. The ingredients used by innovative managers are mixed in widely different proportions depending on the situation, but there are certain basic ones that recur. These include making the job important, involving the worker in the task, communicating what is going on, setting goals together, using promotions creatively, maximizing the benefits of working together, and generating useful profitable suggestions.

Examining these approaches as they are actually applied is far more illuminating than theoretical talk about them, although taking actual cases does not permit the use of tidy categories. Most applications of what has come to be called "job enrichment" are judicious mixtures of the different ingredients, blended to fit the given enterprise, constantly being subtly altered on the basis of experience. Some examples, however, will show what can be accomplished at different levels, and words from the workers themselves will illustrate some of the reactions.

The quintessence of job enrichment in a manufacturing setting occurs when the workers can be given responsibility for an entire operation, with control over setting the pace, doing the job, and testing or examining what they have done. Because of the strictures of many industrial processes, however, it is not often possible to assign the complete task to one worker or team of workers. But the approach to work, and the atmosphere in which it is performed, can be changed radically even in plants that are obliged by the nature of their product to use assembly line techniques.

Making automobile mirrors is one such operation—the glass goes through different steps, successively being coated, cut, polished, mounted, and packed. John F. Donnelly, head of Donnelly Mirrors, Inc., in Holland, Michigan, was an early believer in job improvement. His application of the principle has meant an expanding business, more jobs, and more income for his company. Donnelly took over the company from his father, and ran it from the beginning on the basis of a belief in the worth and dignity of the common man. His common touch was rewarded—not many company presidents get communiqués from their truck drivers—when a Donnelly truck driver back from delivering a load of mirrors reported "something great is going on" at the customer firm. The "something great" interested Donnelly, and when he investigated it, he learned it was an application of the Scanlon Plan for sharing increased earnings from higher productivity with the workers who generate them. Donnelly put a form of the Scanlon Plan into effect, setting up production committees and a screening committee. He gradually developed the concept, with guidance from Dr. Rensis Likert and Dr. Carl Frost, a psychologist, of the University of Michigan.

After an attempt was made to unionize the company in 1960, he set up an employes' committee to handle grievances, wages, and labor relations. The company was growing rapidly, and in 1967 all salaried employes attended a management course, after which work team development activity was accelerated.

To erase, or at least minimize, the distinctions between white-collar and blue-collar workers, hourly rated workers were referred to as "operators," or even "managers," on the premise that they managed their own jobs. Some didn't like this at first, Donnelly says. "It can sound like a gimmick. But now with the work teams, they feel they *really are* managing their work." This sentiment was reenforced when, in 1970, all hourly paid employes were put on salary, so that they are paid even when they miss work. All the time clocks were removed. Absenteeism and tardiness both went down, and people "behaved in an increasingly responsible way," reports Henry Kort, the factory manager.

"Knowing they're doing this," says Mrs. Pat Laarman, twenty-three, a production inspector, "you're more eager and willing to be here because you want to give the fullest cooperation. They're willing to pay you when you're gone, you should be willing to give them full worth." Mrs. Laarman doesn't say it in so many words, but the trusting aspect of the change, with no time clocks and payment of salaries even when workers are absent, has an immediate effect on employes. Suspicion begets suspicion, and trust begets trust.

Donnelly supervisors make intensive, even extraordinary, efforts to keep all hands fully informed both on prospects and problems. This is the kind of communication Stanley Peterfreund urges companies to develop. Sales, production, inventory, and profit charts are prominently displayed in each division of the plant, so those groups know what their objectives should be. Surveys are conducted and questionnaires are distributed frequently, and the results are thoroughly discussed after they have been collated. Detailed articles on new developments and company plans are included in *The Donnelly Mirror,* a glossy-paper monthly published for employes. Division and work team meetings are held frequently; everyone on the payroll is a member of one of them; and everyone knows he is free to speak out. Speak out they do: some workers loudly criticized a management decision—to put up an elaborate panel lighted in colors illustrating company progress—as profligate at the time of a cost-cutting drive. "Could have Xeroxed the information just as good and passed it around," one grumbles. "It's money out of our pockets."

Management listens carefully to what the operators say, and it hears much more than complaints. One maintenance man thought of a way to build a seaming machine, for beveling mirror edges, for only $290, compared to the $900 machine Donnelly would have otherwise bought. His machine was also more adaptable because it could be moved easily.

When the company planned to buy a new glass machine, the production worker who was to run it was taken along with the engineers to visit the manufacturer in California and try it out before making a commitment. The difference between this approach, consulting the worker beforehand, as opposed to confronting him with a piece of new equipment and telling him to run it, is typical of the ways things are done at Donnelly. It takes more time and more planning, to be sure, but the difference in attitudes between the worker whose advice is solicited, and the one whose advice isn't even considered, is worth the effort.

Work teams work hard at, among other things, reducing the number of jobs on a given operation, because they know that with lower production costs and consequent lower prices, sales will flourish, and they will get higher bonuses. The prevailing attitude throughout the plant is that rarely obtained ideal mentioned earlier: one of "we" actively working together, rather than passively following orders coming down from "them."

The changes at Donnelly allowed quality control personnel to be reduced from fifteen to four, although production doubled. The percentage of returned goods declined from 3 percent to two-tenths of 1 percent. In terms of overall growth, the company's sales went from $3.6 million in 1965 to $13.8 million in 1970, and employment went up from 125 to 411 in the same period. Bonuses paid in 1961, when there were already 125 employes, came to $25,000, but by 1970, with worker enthusiasm having its rewarding effects, the bonuses paid to the 411 employes came to $542,000.

An illuminating example of what worker involvement can mean came when the employes, after working out details in their team and division meetings, submitted a request for a pay increase costing $292,000. The company officers agreed, but said, "You'll have to contribute something more. We're not going to add to inflation. Show us how you're going to do it." Within three weeks, management had commitments totaling $636,000 in cost reductions from foremen, department managers, and engineers after work group meetings had discussed areas in which economies could be effected. With this kind of impetus, Donnelly's business not only has grown sharply, but also the cost of its products—70 percent of which is auto mirrors—has gone down each year. Profits have increased an average of 22 percent annually in recent years.

The inside workings of Donnelly's satisfaction-generating machinery were revealed during a meeting of a work group composed of grinders and inspectors from the second shift. Foreman Doug Murr led the discussion, skillfully drawing the quiet ones out, holding talkative ones back so everyone had a chance, explaining patiently and clearly until each person understood. The group talked about the new weekly pay policy. Jane, an inspector, minimized reports that some were taking advantage of the paid absence plan, saying, "I don't feel anyone is taking any money out of my pocket." Gilbert, a grinding machine operator, said gruffly, "More people are sick now—guys who never got sick before get sick now."

Harry, a deep-voiced thoughtful man who pulled steadily on his pipe, spoke slowly. "What if you have to stay home to spray your blueberries? It *is* time to spray your blueberries, isn't it?" he asked, turning to his neighbor. The meeting continued quietly for an hour and a half, with everyone having a chance to be heard. It represented a big investment in man-hours, but the investment quite obviously pays off.

One of the younger workers at Donnelly said the atmosphere at the plant definitely suits him. Ronald Kolean, twenty-five, who runs a glass grinder, says, "Young people here are very satisfied. Just because you are young and out of school, management doesn't look down on you as just a cocky teen-ager. They have just as much respect for any employe, regardless of age."

Across the country, in a business that is quite different, use of a similar approach has allowed another small company to make similarly profitable improvements. At Precision Castparts Corporation, in Portland, Oregon, enlisting worker enthusiasm has allowed the small foundry firm to stay competitive with its more strategically located rivals, in a fearsomely competitive business. Again the decision to make changes that would engage the employes in furthering the company's business was made by the chief executive. At Precision Castparts, President Edward Cooley determined to introduce job enrichment after being himself exposed to the thinking of several behavioral scientists. Cooley began the process of change by holding talks with every production worker in the plant, and learned to his surprise that some employes felt their jobs were no better than being in jail or back in high school. As part of the effort to get the workers to involve themselves, the different departments were organized into teams, whose members discussed their production goals and the methods they would use to reach them. By consulting those who were expected to do the work on what was feasible and how it could be accomplished, the managers got real participation from the employes. In fact, the job was actually managed by the workers—and when they are their own bosses, they are tougher than some foremen. When Cooley first became interested in improving jobs at Precision Castparts, the main emphasis was placed on the wax assembly section, which included around thirty-five people, mostly women. Several teams were created to work on cost reduction, and task forces figured out their own production goals. One result was that the section workers got together and decided to stop rotation from one machine to another each day. The rotation had caused problems. Productivity went up sharply, from $110 per hour worked to $135. Further loosening of restrictions, under an "individual freedoms and responsibilities" program, allowing people to set their own hours and make other decisions, caused productivity to increase further, from $135 per hour to $210 per hour in four months. At the same time, morale improved and absenteeism dropped.

After job enrichment had been in effect for a while, the ideas for solving production problems, in what is an intricate and complex process, began flowing in. One worker figured out a way to improve pressure control in the wax molding phase of the casting process by using a $9 automobile jack. In another section, where the wax molds are cleaned, another worker's suggestion allowed management to cut supervisors from two to one.

The general level of worker interest rose sharply. Casting parts is a tricky process, fraught with hazards and mystery because much of what happens cannot be seen by the operators—it all goes on inside the mold. Failed castings cost as much to make as perfect ones, but the failure can only be detected when the casting has been completed—and the failures bring no revenue. The complexity of the parts now being routinely cast adds to the difficulties. But by changing procedures so that workers have become personally involved in the production process and its success, Precision Castparts reduced its reject rate from 24 percent to 7 percent between 1965 and 1970.

One worker at Precision Castparts expresses it this way: "We can move around now and get information on a project without going through our leads. This saves time and means information is firsthand. It saves mistakes to get it direct." For their parts, managers benefit because they have more time to really manage, rather than using their time with low-level problem-solving that doesn't require their expertise.

Another worker made these comments on the changed atmosphere at Precision Castparts: "You enjoy getting up and going to work—you get recognition here; that feeds the ego, and the ego feeds production. No one is hovering over you. We can make decisions. There is more responsibility to the individual."

One aspect of job improvement that causes confusion and, sometimes, disagreement, is that of terminology. The growth of interest in job enrichment, as workers have shown greater reluctance to engage themselves in their jobs, has led to a proliferation of approaches to the problem, and to some genteel, academic-type competition among the professors and consultants. This, in turn, has allowed the emergence of what Frederick Herzberg, of Case Western Reserve University, a leading figure in the motivation field, delicately calls "sellers of snake oil." Herzberg maintains, not surprisingly, that his own theory, which distinguishes between motivating factors and mere maintenance factors that do not motivate, is the one and only revealed truth about job improvement. A good many companies have indicated they believe him. Herzberg decries the "whole bunch of nondescript behavioral scientists who are selling love and sitting around in groups with their clothes on. They have borrowed a lot of my ideas, mixed them around, and made a stew. Some companies are actually carrying out fraud: they are just doing attitudinal change. Delegation is not job enrichment. It's letting somebody borrow your job for a while."

The rush to conform, which so often plagues America in so many ways, has led some companies to embrace job enrichment overenthusiastically, often prematurely. The sudden interest has some of the unfortunate aspects of a fad, with its concomitant qualities of excess and poor judgment. Danger signals management should watch for when seeking outside advice are a weakness for cant and an air of mysticism with an accompanying inability to explain specifics, which the seer expects the customer to accept on blind faith. If they can't say it in intelligible English, it probably means it isn't worth saying, or that they don't understand it themselves.

Most frightening, perhaps, for managements hesitant to embark on job improvement or enrichment, is the absence of any clearly outlined model to follow. But companies going into job enrichment have to be prepared to grope, to explore, to fail, before reaching the goals they seek. Dr. Edwin Land, who has made the creation of rewarding jobs a central objective of his Polaroid Corporation, says of the risk involved, "Our greatest contribution [in job enrichment] has been to learn how to fail without guilt. The scientific notion is that you can fail, and fail, and fail, before you succeed. We are trying to apply this scientific attitude of tolerating failure to the social innovations we are trying here in the plant."

The Corning Glass Works went into job enrichment with the guidance of a staff professional, Dr. Michael Beer, and applied it at a small plant that then had 50, and now has 120, employes, where the risks were comparatively small. The plant is in Medfield, Massachusetts, where the company manufactures scientific equipment and instruments. Dr. Beer uses the term *organizational development* to describe the approach he and the executives of his company take, because the overall goal is to apply the best of a variety of behavioral science concepts about effective management, not limiting the innovations to participative management and job enrichment.

At the Medfield plant, an assembly line on which six women worked together assembling different elements of a laboratory hot plate was eliminated and each of the women was charged with assembling complete units, from start to finish. This made for a much longer work cycle for each worker, since the plates took about thirty minutes to put together. The women were also asked to put their initials on the finished hot plates, both to give them personal identification with the products and to allow any customer complaints to reach the right person. Scheduling was arranged by the workers, not by supervisors, and was paced to meet weekly or monthly goals. Each member of the group, and the group as a whole, was encouraged to suggest ideas for designing the work stations and improving them.

After this approach had been well established, the women were given greater responsibility for quality assurance. Until then, the quality assurance department had checked every hot plate, but with the change, the assemblers checked their own work, and only sample checks were performed by quality assurance. This too increased identification with the product by the workers. In effect, Corning was saying, "No one is looking over your shoulder—we count on you to do it right." The sharp reduction of quality assurance checks also allowed reducing the personnel in that department, permitting significant savings. As Dr. Beer sums up the several changes, they broadened "the scope, and therefore the meaningfulness of the job. Delegation of scheduling to the workers increased the planning component, as did the assignment of total assembly. Since each hot plate assembly was under the complete control of one single girl, she could plan to change her approach to the job on her own. The quality assurance responsibility and the identification of the individual who assembled the hot plate increased the control component in the job."

The results of these comparatively modest changes, which involved no new equipment and in fact allowed reducing personnel because fewer inspectors were used, were striking. In the six months following the change controllable rejects dropped from 23 percent to 1 percent, and absenteeism dropped from 8 percent to 1 percent. During the same time period, productivity in the department increased despite transfers of personnel in and out of the department, and despite the fact that there was no major process improvement. An intangible, but important, ancillary benefit was that the reputation of the hot plate department changed from that of a bad place to work to a good place.

Some time after the hot plate changes had been proven valid, and other improvements had been made, similar changes were made in the method of assembly of a complex measuring instrument called a digital electrometer, one model of which costs $1,800. The department making these instruments was restructured into two work groups, each of which had complete responsibility for the assembly of instruments, scheduling, work assignment, quality assurance, and even the delicate and crucial task of calibration. Here too important efforts were made to get worker participation in design of the jobs, and in the layout of the department. Setting group goals resulted in a higher degree of personal involvement with the achievement of those goals, and made workers try to get the approval of their fellows by doing their full share of the work.

One Corning worker at the Medfield plant appraises the changes this way: "I'm doing a better job. I just like this place so much, I just think it's wonderful. I've never worked in a place where we've had so much closeness with supervisors."

Other comments, gathered by Dr. Beer, include these:

"I am now interested in the team and what we can do as a team in terms of our goal. Sometimes I sit at home and think of how we can better the goal, whether we'll make the goal, and how we can improve the goals."

"You get involved in your job here and won't stay home because you have a goal to meet."

"We started teams and you really know what you have to do. No one has to tell you what to do next, and it helps us to use our time better. They should have it this way in all of the different departments throughout the plant. The supervisors praise you here and you work more here because you are praised. Praise brings more work."

"Since I've been working at Medfield, my husband is a much better supervisor in his plant. I tell him what he should do to make his people more interested in what they are doing based on what our supervisors do here."

"I love it. I can't get over how tremendous it is, and after all the time I've been here, I still go home to my husband at night and do nothing but rave about it because it's mostly the nature and the freedom of the relationships between the people throughout the plant from the plant manager on down. Everyone is so tremendous. They seem friendly, interested, and concerned about us. I also feel that I know everything that's going on in the plant and feel this is very important. It makes things a lot more interesting to understand what is happening and I like going to the meetings and finding out what's happening to the plant sales."

Dr. Beer is well aware that the smallness of the plant made experimentation and change far easier than it would have been in a huge, old factory with thousands of employes. The nature of the work done at Medfield made it easier to change things than if elaborate modifications of equipment had been required, with big investments and high risks. Beer also had the benefit of coming in by invitation of the plant personnel supervisor, at a time when procedures were under reexamination and it was intended to make a variety of changes in any case.

A critical reader will at this point acknowledge, per-

haps, that such changes can be made in some plants, and
that they can be made to work, and to produce good
results. But the same reader will point out that it is often
the very worst jobs, the jobs that are hardest to improve,
that engender the most discontent. Jobs such as the
messy, smelly, disagreeable ones in slaughterhouses, service jobs such as garbage removal, and certain industrial
jobs such as those in foundries and on auto assembly
lines.

Such an observation is quite correct, but while it is
true that some jobs are harder to improve than others,
almost no job is immune to improvement. Take the
doleful task of the dishwasher in a restaurant, for example. Thirty years ago the job was done by hand, by a
man or woman standing in puddles of water, bending
over a steaming sink, handling each plate and glass and
fork individually, for hours on end, with minimal pay
and no social standing whatsoever. Now, the job has
been improved. Machinery does most of it, the hours are
better, the pay higher; and as one result, even the standing of the dishwasher is improved. Similarly, garbage
men have dirty, dangerous jobs low in prestige and certainly low in satisfactions. But these too have been improved: garbage is being compacted or mashed into fra-
grance-free bundles, or collected in metal bins that are
dumped directly into trucks without the garbage man
ever touching them. In one Florida town garbage is collected from side streets by men driving scooters with
dump mechanisms, an innovation that has improved
productivity and reduced turnover. In New York city
garbage men have a title, "sanitation worker," and a

uniform, and get frequent public assurance that their jobs are of high importance. Even those jobs, then, have been improved.

# chapter

# 6

# *Resolving Rather Than Temporizing*

Imaginative executives like those at Corning Glass and Precision Castparts have been able to make truly significant changes in the jobs performed by their workers—with the wholehearted cooperation of those workers themselves. But making the assembly line at an auto plant a daily joy for those who work there is a more difficult challenge and one that has resisted many studies and experiments. Automobile building requires large quantities of men, materials, and power, and a lot of space for the lines, for equipment, for stocking parts, and for storing the assembled cars. This in turn means a big capital investment that must be kept productive if its owners are to get an adequate return on their money. The pace of the assembly line must be kept uniform, and it must move as quickly as possible without introducing

109

too high a rate of defects. Everything is pushed to its limits, and the pushing is done by impersonal, remote machine rather than by the worker's own decision. There is no such thing as finishing early on an automobile assembly line.

While they may be reluctant to introduce sweeping changes because of the economic imperatives mentioned, the men who run the car business are intensely aware of the problems facing them, as Roche's and Cole's speeches show, and they have made various attempts to improve jobs. Given the immutable aspects of car assembly, these attempts have had to be less than sweeping, and certainly none of them has resulted in an over-all, fundamental solution. But efforts are being made.

General Motors has experimented with a variety of approaches in different sectors of its huge establishment. One tactic was the frontal assault by its top executives on poor attendance and insufficient increases in productivity. This attack did not bring with it a solution, but if nothing else, it brought the problem out into the open, where it could be examined, and where at least some workers and union officials would have to acknowledge the facts. Delineation of the problem can be a significant step in seeking a solution.

General Motors is also trying to increase its corporate understanding of the reasons for its problems with its workers. Dr. Delmar L. Landen, GM's director of employe research, who has a doctorate in psychology and fourteen years' experience with the company, agrees with other experts that the company's labor difficulties rise essentially from the high hopes and aspirations of youth. "People are entering society with a set of expectations predicated on affluence and education. What's happening in industry is a microcosm of what is happening on campuses and in the civil rights movement."

Relating the changes to the hierarchical levels of satisfaction established in Maslow's work, Landen says, "People who came through the Depression and World War II cling more to values at the security-need level." Younger workers, unscarred by memories of the Depression, have other requirements, and "when they see the incongruity between what they *want* and what they can expect in an auto plant, one solution for them is to quit."

Earlier attempts to deal with industrial manpower problems, Landen recalls, included the efficiency approach, followed by the human relations approach. "Now," he says, "where we have to aim is participation —it is the only way to work in this increasingly complex society. The man at the top can't have all the answers. The man doing the job will have some of them." (The concept is not limited to the United States. "Participation," as pronounced with a French accent, was a central element in the efforts of Charles de Gaulle to assuage working-class discontent in France during the latter years of his presidency.)

Reflecting the change of attitude in some executive offices in Detroit, Landen cites the social psychologists to back up his views, something that would not have gone down very well in the car business a few years earlier. The automobile industry, he says, "assumed economic man was served if the pay was okay; it didn't matter if the job was fulfilling. Now, once the pay is good, higher Maslow values come into play," other satisfactions are required. The reason auto production workers in West Germany and Japan still work as dedicatedly as they do, Landen says, "is because they are still at a lower point on the Maslow scale; they are more concerned with basic needs and security." Also, he says, the authority-compliance structure is quite different in Japan and Germany from that in the U.S.

Various methods of dealing with absenteeism and job discontent have been suggested by managers and theoreticians, ranging from leaving the jobs as dull as they are and hiring dull men to fill them, to automating the plants completely, throwing out the old assembly line in the process, and eliminating the dull jobs altogether. Both extremes seem to be ruled out, one because it ignores basic human values, the other because the technology, while theoretically possible, would cost so much that the cars could not be sold. The more central course many advocate would have managers find ways to make jobs varied and interesting through motivational and technological approaches. This admittedly is a tall order. Some GM plants, groping for a solution, have even tried rewarding regular attendance with Green Stamps, or initialed glasses that over the months (of regular attendance, of course) form a set.

Whatever is done, Landen emphasizes, it must be remembered that absenteeism and allied problems are only symptoms of trouble, not causes. Of his search for a cure, he admits that as of now, "We don't have the answers." But, he says, "one thing is sure: if they won't come in for $30.50 a day, they won't come in for a monogrammed glass." His overall view, as he studies the situation, is optimistic, and seems to signal a new outlook in the executive offices of the biggest industry of the United States. "We are having very vital, critical changes in our society," he says, "and the question is how we can capitalize on this, how we can exploit the forces of change and profit from them rather than suffering from them."

One forward-looking approach to improving auto assembly jobs is that being used at GM's plant in Lordstown, Ohio, where the low-cost Vega 2300 was put into production in 1970. The production line there includes various refinements aimed at making the jobs easier; for example, the Vega chassis is raised and lowered automatically as it moves along the line, to speed assembly and make the workers' job easier. Because labor input must be reduced if GM is to make a profit building these smaller cars, every phase of the assembly operation was restudied, and much of it was redesigned. The line itself is designed to move at one hundred cars an hour, compared with the usual fifty-five, surpassing even the ninety-one Oldsmobiles built each hour at Lansing. This sounds at first blush as though management is imposing a real speedup—the rapid pace has caused some complaints and disruption—but in fact it should not mean that the men on the line work any harder; the specific assembly jobs are simply broken up differently, with different time spans allocated for each.

Some have suggested, half-seriously, that the solution to the anguish of the assembly line is to have each car built individually by one man, who would do the whole job, making the engine, welding the chassis, assembling the body, and so on. While this concept has a certain artisanal charm, the cost of such cars would range somewhere up in the tens of thousands of dollars. A moderately individualistic approach is taken toward each car at the Ferrari works in Italy, for example, and at Rolls-Royce in England, and the cars produced in those ateliers, while splendid, cost from $12,000 to $30,000.

On the technological side, inventors and engineers are continually studying ways to automate the automobile assembly process more fully. Mechanical robots can be designed and built to perform almost any job that men or women do along the assembly line. The difficulty here is the cost of such devices, and their lack of flexibility. Modern plants run a tremendous variety of cars representing different models and options along the same production lines. Because of this variety, it is cheaper, gruesome as it sounds, for management to pay men to do the jobs required on each car, varying slightly as they do from one model or style to another, than it would be to develop, program, build, and install sophisticated robots to do those same jobs. Even today, visits to competing automobile · companies reveal that operations done by machine at one company are done by workers at another. Certain body welding operations, for example, can be done either by machine or by workers, and it is a managerial decision at which point the trade-offs of cost in machinery and costs in human terms balance out. But doing body welds or chassis welds all day long during an eight-hour shift, performing the same operation every seventy seconds, doing the same set of motions 348 times in all, with coffee and lunch breaks the only interruptions, does not, as Walter Reuther put it, "lift the human spirit."

Engineers continue studying the possibilities of breaking auto building into components that can be put together by groups of workers. This offers two advantages. The workers can work at more or less their own pace, as long as they keep the components moving and meet the production goal for their shift. And by breaking elements of the car into subassemblies, the final assembly job is made simpler, and repairs after the car is in service can be made more readily. Some cars are now made with complete dashboard and instrument cluster assemblies, ready to plug in to one or more master cable harnesses in one motion. The crews that make the instrument cluster-dash assemblies work in areas off the noisy assembly line, can trade jobs with each other, speed up to get ahead so they can take a break, and enjoy a greater degree of camaraderie with their fellows than is possible on the fast-moving main line.

This approach, which has been used in United States auto plants for some time, is being refined in Sweden, where both Volvo and Saab-Scania are using teams. In one application, men doing different assembly operations move along the production line at the same pace as the cars, rather than having men at fixed stations perform the same operation on each car as it goes by. In addition, the factories are using the team approach to production of subassemblies or components, with the groups deciding in what order to proceed, changing jobs if they wish, even electing their own leader. Job rotation is also used, with workers doing different jobs on the cars from one day to the next.

A problem in this kind of experiment is that while some workers welcome the daily change or other variations, there are always a certain number who stubbornly

resist such approaches. These workers find a good deal
of comfort in an unvarying routine and dislike, sometimes even fear, the challenge of doing a different job.
"I can just turn my mind off once I get started," one
such worker says. "I don't mind doing the same thing—
I don't even have to think about it." Managers have to
try to reconcile the wish of many workers to have variety
and change with the reluctance of these more placid
souls, and this brings in new complications.

One place management has looked for assistance in
improving attendance and performance by workers is to
the union. This has been done in the belief that because
it is the union with which management negotiates the
terms on which its members work, the union has some
responsibility for obliging members to perform their
agreed-upon duties reliably and conscientiously. Feelings among union officials about union responsibilities
in this area are divided, however. Some unionists say
flatly they have no interest in furthering the accomplishments of management's goals. A management appeal of
this sort puts the union in a difficult position: it is supposed to be the unswerving advocate and defender of its
dues-paying members, and yet, as some auto executives
see things, it is supposed to help management enforce
work discipline, somewhat the way a medieval guild
might have done. Some younger union members are already dubious about the close ties between older union
leaders—the age gap shows again here—and management. Appeals from management to the union to press
the members to meet company requirements or standards confirms their suspicion that union and manage-

ment are allied.

Because the most frequent point of contact between company and worker is made through the foreman, on the plant floor, this is an area in which improvements can logically be sought. On the average, there is one foreman to every thirty production workers, and the majority of the foremen have come up from the hourly ranks, so most of them know the problems, know their men, and know how to talk with them. Recognizing this, each of the big three auto makers operates training programs for their foremen designed to increase their effectiveness as leaders. Pontiac takes production foremen off on two-day weekend seminars to a lakeside resort for some specially tailored sensitivity training and discussion of problems new workers face, along with possible solutions. Chrysler has a special consultant who works with its foremen, stressing the difficulties faced by disadvantaged minority group members when they start work in an auto plant.

On a broader level, General Motors has operated a New Work Force program for its executives and some supervisors in plants across the country since late 1968. The title was chosen to indicate General Motors's awareness that there is indeed a new and different work force, with different characteristics, which is not made up only of hard core, or disadvantaged, or black people, but of all kinds of people. It includes whites, older people, younger people, persons with less education and of different cultures, some with criminal records, many who would once have been considered unemployable. The program gives managers a look at the lives of such workers, takes some of them into ghetto areas, puts them in role-playing situations where they act out the workers' parts in interviews dealing with absenteeism, discipline, and orientation on a new job. Supervisors are shown how to reduce new employes' tensions, because it is these tensions that, if unresolved, can cause them to leave, stay out of work, or rebel in some other fashion.

The shock of starting work in the noise and constant movement of an auto assembly plant turns a lot of new employes off from the moment they report on their first day. Ford executives moved to mitigate this shock by commissioning a film, made in cinéma vérité style, aimed at new employes and designed to show them what production work is really like, so that when they step out on the clangorous floor on that first day of work, they won't be dismayed. It has an unusual title, *Don't Paint It Like Disneyland,* and as a Ford official says, "It's an unusual industrial film. We don't have the chairman of the board giving a speech about working for Ford, either at the beginning or at the end." It is unusual too in its frankness. One production worker says, "It's a drag at first but you realize you got to do it, so you do it." Another looks up from his job on the line, says in a puzzled way, "I got a good job—but it's pretty bad." Ford also conducts human relations programs at various plants that in effect constitute sensitivity training and guide supervisors in dealing with motivation, work control, costs, and quality.

Conversations with foremen and visits to different plants indicate that the message conveyed in these different kinds of leadership sessions for supervisors is getting through to them, whether or not it is to the workers. Reflecting the change from the authoritarianism of ten years ago to the persuasion of today, one chassis assembly foreman at Cadillac says, "I try to work *with* them, not threaten them. The old type tactics of being a supervisor don't work with these guys. In the past a man didn't need much motivation to do a job like this—the paycheck took care of that. But these guys—they're different!" A foreman in the foundry division at Pontiac says, "I try not to use the discipline route. I tell the man the pocketbook effect on him. Some of this absenteeism is for simple reasons, like the foreman didn't smile right or turned his back when you were talking, or family reasons, the wife is sick. I've been threatened, every foreman out there has been threatened, I've had a couple of threats to be killed over firings." (When production executives call foremen the "front line of management," they mean it in the combat as well as the administrative sense.) "I get questioned on assignments, but I try to anticipate the questions and explain *why*. That way if he wants to argue, he has to meet me head-on."

There are other techniques for generating and maintaining employes' interest and involvement in their jobs. General Motors runs a vigorous, well-financed suggestion program that in one recent year alone brought in 324,647 ideas for ways to do things more efficiently or save time and money. The company adopted 279,461 of them, and paid more than $17 million to the suggesters. Ford is also looking hard for ways to give workers more feeling of responsibility and authority in their work. One tactic being applied at its Wayne assembly plant is an established technique with a new name. It is called the "positive-buy" inspection. The inspector signs his name on the inspection sheet for each car he passes. This indicates personal approval, makes the inspector feel he is a person rather than a number, and, in theory at least, ensures active examination rather than passive acceptance. Various plant managers are experimenting with other approaches to improving motivation, such as job rotation, group or teamwork, and self-set or group-set quotas, like the methods being tried out in Sweden.

A case history illustrating the use of different methods in a series of escalating steps was offered by the General Motors assembly plant in Baltimore, where absenteeism had gone up steadily from 3 percent in 1966 to 6.9 percent three years later, and continued climbing in 1970 to 8 percent. Management tried a whole array of tactics. The basic approach was through the foremen, who were taught that they have the fundamental responsibility to the employe for assurance of his safety, getting him time off for personal business when necessary, and for his job training. They were told to make every effort to know their workers as individuals, and to try to make them want to work. In another type of attack on the absentee problem, workers needing time off were urged to ask in advance, so that management could plan ahead to let them off and replace them. The difficulty there was that not all the requests could always be granted—for example, during Maryland's deer season, when everyone wants to be off—and refusal sometimes seemed to create as much resentment as the restriction on absence itself.

The next stage beyond motivation, foreman initiatives, and excused absences was what Baltimore plant management terms "the discipline route." One worker says the foremen were definitely "under pressure from management," and as a result, "they tightened the reins on the workers." Union officials confirmed that there was a discipline clampdown in an effort to keep absenteeism from climbing still further. More men were given "time off," (meaning disciplinary suspensions from work without pay), more reprimands and dismissals were handed out. One Friday on the second shift (3:30 P.M. to midnight) in April 1970 there were more than two hundred employes absent, of the shift force of twenty-seven hundred hourly workers. Friday absenteeism often runs high because the men like to stitch together three-day weekends, and because second shift workers are paid Thursday, by union demand, so they don't have to come in Friday to get their money. Management decided to shut down the plant after just four hours, a decision that meant that those who *had* come to work lost half a day's pay, through no fault of their own. The union cried foul, claiming management took the absenteeism as a money-saving excuse to cut production because of lower sales. Dozens of workers canceled their U.S. Savings Bond and Community Chest deductions, both ardently advocated by the company, to show their displeasure and to get back at management. H. H. Prentice, the plant manager, had letters mailed to every worker, addressed "Dear Fellow-Employee and Family," explaining why the closing was necessary, urging "your best effort in being at work every day on time," and expressing certainty that "most of our employes want to be at work every day to provide for themselves and their families." Thus to the "discipline route" was added the "family route." With cooperation from employes, Prentice ended his letter, "we will avoid the necessity of harsh disciplinary measures." The threat seemed sufficiently clear.

The automobile industry is thus trying a variety of different approaches at various plants, ranging from sensitivity training to tough crackdowns, from persuasion to bribery, but so far it has not overcome the fundamental obstacle to rewarding work that is constituted by the assembly line.

In white-collar jobs, the problem of job improvement has certain curious parallels with the situation in car factories, in that there is a steady and heavy flow of work, and the jobs are often quite impersonal, permitting little involvement. The term "paper factories," sometimes used to describe the big offices where forms are mass-processed or bills tabulated, often has a certain unhappy accuracy. This is one reason for the decline in morale among white-collar workers.

Because white-collar workers have higher expectations for themselves and of their jobs, one of the most effective tools management can use in retaining their interest in their jobs is promotion. In conversations with dozens of white-collar workers in all sorts of jobs, the most significant common thread running through their comments—especially among the younger ones—was the expectation of and requirement for quick, frequent promotions. Some of them sounded like school kids talking of what they'd be doing next year; they were as certain of promotion as high school students are of the automatic promotions given them to keep them moving through and out of school. The appeal of white-collar jobs is no longer the security they used to offer, nor is it the status they used to give the holder. It is certainly not the big money that attracts. It is advancement that appeals, and the promotions do not even necessarily have to bring an immediate pay raise with them, as long as they broaden the worker's responsibility or authority or autonomy.

Lawrence Porto, nineteen, a First National City Bank teller in New York, who got his job at the first place he applied and had had three major promotions in his two-year career, attends banking courses at night, and confidently expects to be running a branch office of his own one day. "It's how well you do the job," he says. "They notice you, and you just move up." When he first started, as a check sorter, he wasn't sure how good the promotion prospects were, but then, "I found there was more to the job than I saw at first, more opportunity, after I was there awhile, and talked to people, and saw how they progressed. In six months I went up to clearance clerk. There was more money and responsibility. That was when I started liking it and planned to stay."

"Those companies which have thought in terms of careers, which have counselors available, which practice job posting, which have thought of progression—they seem to be on the right track," says Harvard Professor Fred K. Foulkes. Visits to companies that operate this way, and talks with their employes, bear out the importance of promotions, and bring out some other values too. General Mills, Inc., with more than $1 billion in sales and twenty-six thousand employes worldwide, sounds like a place in which an employe could easily become lost. But the company has a turnover of only 18 percent at its Minneapolis home office, compared to the 30 percent average local turnover figure. Art Brown, its personnel director, explains the good showing this way: "We make a studied effort to place people where they'll be most effective, and move them if this is indicated. We offer training to employes so they feel they can advance, that they have an opportunity for professional growth. It is satisfying for them to know they can expand their horizons."

General Mills has applied new approaches in the newest major area of white-collar jobs, its data processing operations. One such tactic simultaneously trains employes in advanced data processing and resolves the problem of staffing the undesirable late shifts that have to be worked to make economically effective use of the big expensive computers. Its solution is to recruit young men and women who want to work their way through college. The company lets late-shift employes work shorter hours, so they can attend university classes during the day and work toward their degrees. General Mills pays the tuition. By so doing, it fills the late-shift slots, gets a continuing upgrading of its computer staff, and develops loyalty among persons who can be expected to stay with General Mills when they have completed their campus educations.

General Mills has also eliminated most repetitive paperwork jobs, and upgraded the remaining ones. The company has been able, as a spokesman put it in a metaphor particularly apt for a food company, to "take things in bite-sized chunks." Its director of management systems and data processing, Robert M. Weller, says the company began planning its mechanization in 1954, and that "we have eliminated many of the routine statistical, accounting, records, and billing jobs since then. We now have many fewer jobs, but more good jobs. Without electronic data processing we would have 500 persons, earning $350 to $400 a month, handling these operations. Instead we have 140 earning $400 to $500, and 70 systems and programs people earning $10,000 to $12,000 a year. So we have reduced the number of jobs, increased the pay and the satisfactions, and yet we are handling four or five times the business and volume of fifteen years ago. We can also provide management with information for decisions that we simply could not have furnished before."

General Mills has no hesitation about putting young people in charge of areas in which they have shown competence; youth is no barrier to such advancement. And while younger people may lack some of the perspective and experience older persons have, they can sometimes obtain better performance from the young people working under them. A young supervisor at General Mills, Daryl Delzer, who had worked up to mailing department supervisor at the age of twenty-four after beginning as a mail clerk six years earlier, illustrates the receptivity that youth affords youth. He says he enjoys working with young people because "they ask 'why' a lot, and that sharpens the thinking for the supervisor. It makes you stop and think about methods. They're not the way people think, they're not against the establishment. They are testing you. It means you'd better have thought about things first, before telling them what to do."

In Atlanta, the Retail Credit Company, the largest credit-information business in the country, with thirteen thousand clerical, administrative, and field employes, has made job advancement the central armature of its corporate philosophy. Its president, W. Lee Burge, says, "In the 1970s our objective is to provide a good career, to create additional employment and promotional opportunities for our people, to challenge individual abilities, and to foster an even better climate for personal development." Burge should know what promotion can mean; he worked his way up from a beginning job in Retail Credit's mail room in 1936. One of his employes, Jim Slade, a computer programmer who at thirty had two years with the company and was thinking ahead, saw things in much the same way, looking at the company from the other end of the telescope. He says he expects to be in management within ten years, and that he particularly likes the emphasis on promotions from within. He says he thinks Retail Credit is a superior company because it has "outstanding management people—and that's because they train their own."

The question of training is inextricably linked with promotion, as Slade's remark suggests. That question becomes particularly relevant when the business is in a major urban center such as New York. The First National City Bank offers an example of what can be done. Because of the nature of the labor supply available, the kind of work it does, and the need to provide continuing possibilities for promotions, First National City has to run its own school system with a variety of courses ranging from secretarial skills through beginning level banking to managerial level instruction. The bank's school system is as large as those of some small towns, with more than six thousand employes taking courses each year at a new, specially built complex in Queens. The center has a training and education staff of one hundred, and its elaborate equipment, including computer-assisted instruction, closed-circuit television, and video tape recorders, cost $800,000. (The bank also operates two street academies, and makes other banking, management, and college courses available.)

"The city schools are not preparing young people in New York for the business world, either in the use of business equipment, or in attitude," says Norman Willard, First National City's director of training. "Problems of employe performance—error rate, promptness, and the like, we attribute these to the deterioration of the school system. The reading level of new employes is down, and although this should not be a bank problem, we have to run remedial courses." A side benefit to the training courses, helping to balance the cost, is lower turnover. Employes realize that with the training made available, they can learn valuable skills, and that they can move up rapidly within the bank. Mary L. Brown, in her early twenties, a key punch operator at First National City, says she thinks she could probably get more varied work and higher pay in a smaller office, but that she likes the bank job because of the training program.

The impact of the computer on white-collar jobs has a strange duality, which is illustrated at First National City Bank. In some cases computers prove a boon by eliminating drudge jobs and creating more promotion opportunity, but in others they narrow the task demands and make for dull, boring, repetitive jobs. In banking, there are special paper-handling problems, because personal checks are still central to the business and their handwritten entries cannot be read by machine. This situation will be resolved when the checkless phase of banking comes to pass, with all transactions handled by computers and initiated with a coded personal card. But, until then, as Robert Feagles, First National City senior vice-president, says, "One and a half to two million checks per day have to be handled by individuals, despite scanners and other devices. Imagine sitting at a machine all day, reading the amounts and punching the amounts into a machine. Try and make *that* person believe he or she is part of the banking system, the vast monetary system that makes this country function!

"As they say in Oklahoma," Feagles continues, "you're caught in a Weewoka switch, a schizophrenic position, because you've got to break jobs down to simple elements in view of the lower quality of some workers available to you, but you at the same time want to make the jobs more challenging."

The problem of operating in a major city, and drawing on it for a labor supply, is compounded by the challenge of the new generation of big-city white-collar workers. These workers are different from those of the past in other ways besides their diminished sense of the old work ethic and their lower effective level of schooling. There has been a sharp change from the years just after World War II, when employes resisted and resented any intrusion on their lives by the company that employed them. "Then, it was 'Stay out of my life,' " says

Feagles of the FNCB, where more than one-third of the employes are from minority groups. "Now, with the sad state of society, with family, religion, and the schools all disqualified, the job and the employer become central. The employer is almost the last resort now, the company is the only entity that is not disqualified." As a result, companies in big cities find themselves not only teaching reading, writing, and arithmetic, but giving lessons in comportment and dress, and providing family counseling and medical care. They almost serve in loco parentis, which, oddly enough, is just what university students have been struggling to abolish on campuses. So totally do employes rely on their companies in places such as New York City that on the first day that abortion restrictions were lifted in New York State, the medical department of one big firm got a telephone call asking if an employe could get an abortion at the office.

Some companies admit frankly that they try to do more for young workers from minority groups who are ill prepared for the world of work than they do for others without special problems. The approach is similar in its reasoning and its intent to that taken by colleges and universities that relax admissions standards for less-qualified minority applicants or give them special training outside classes. Edward Robie, senior vice-president for personnel of the Equitable Life Assurance Society in New York, says, regarding less-qualified minority employes: "There is a problem here. We try, but we can't move minority-group employes ahead as fast as we would like to. We have tried to open up employment opportunities, but a large number of the people available to us are very poorly educated in reading and writing, and our supervisors are used to getting the work done in a certain way, by handing along written instructions. Now they have to show them. Also, they have a different life-style, they are more relaxed, less prone to hop to it when they get an order." Part of the solution lies in training, and part of it is in improving supervisor-worker communications, which should get better, Robie says, "as we get more supervisors from the minority groups."

The same sort of compassionate thinking prevails in the offices of the federal government, the largest employer of white-collar workers in the country. Leo R. Werts, then assistant secretary of labor for administration, said, "Certainly we practice reverse discrimination with minorities. We discriminate in reverse on a lot of people—we have preferential treatment for women in some jobs, and for veterans. We discriminate in reverse to accomplish purposes the country feels should be accomplished."

The company with the most extensive experience in the U.S. in improving white-collar jobs is the American Telephone and Telegraph Company. Through some of its subsidiary telephone companies, Robert N. Ford, personnel director for manpower development and utilization, conducted nineteen job-improvement trials based on Dr. Frederick Herzberg's "work itself" concept. In one, the Indiana Bell Telephone Company, Inc., changed its directory compilation procedures so that each girl took complete responsibility for every step in producing one of the books, from scheduling to final proofreading. Before the changes, there was a production line, with seventeen separate operations for each of the yellow pages, so that no one person felt responsible, knowing checkers would check on the checkers. The changes were introduced over several months, to avoid shock. When the new work assignments had been in effect for a year, force losses dropped from twenty-eight to twenty, error rates declined, absenteeism was lower, and fewer overtime hours were required.

AT&T has conducted other trials at Ford's urging in almost every kind of telephone job, from frameman to engineer to operator to service representative, in different parts of the country. One of the most striking improvements was registered in Pacific Telephone's Los Angeles Central area, mentioned earlier, where in 1969 turnover among operators reached 64.6 percent, and the traffic division had to recruit, hire, and train 1,699 new operators at the cost of $1 million. Lenz Meylan, division traffic manager, calculated that after six to nine months—a point at which many operators grow tired of the job and leave—the company had had an adequate return on its training investment. He therefore initiated a policy of promoting operators into service representative jobs—better paid and with more prestige—instead of hiring the representatives from outside. In just thirty weeks, 150 persons were promoted, and there was a sharp improvement in quality of persons applying for operator jobs because of the new promotion potential. Meylan gave his district managers a goal of reducing turnover by 20 percent and got $100,000 of the department's budget committed to the job improvement effort, which went far toward convincing doubters that the company was really serious.

Partial results for 1970 showed an improvement of 38.9 percent in retaining operators, which meant hiring 285 fewer people from January through August, which in turn meant a saving of $145,000.

Mrs. Marsha Milang, a twenty-three-year-old service representative, says she is pleased with the changes in the Los Angeles office, because "a year ago you didn't know how you were doing; now when there is a good feedback, the feeling is good. You can say, 'Oh boy, I'm really doing something good.' I didn't understand 'work itself' when I first came here, but now I know that it is a program for developing decision-making abilities. The supervisors are letting out more line and giving more freedom without approval being required. They're giving us more responsibility and it's rewarding. We are the persons"—and she summed her job up in a telling phrase—"between the customer and the computer."

For management to reduce the level of discontent among workers requires that the managers know what aspects of the jobs irritate the employes, and this in turn requires communication. There is downward communication, by which management lets the employes know about the company's objectives and problems, and where it is heading. And there is the reverse flow of communication, getting the word up from the employes to the executives. When Najeeb Halaby, then newly appointed as president of Pan American World Airways, contemplated the year ahead after taking office, with the all-important introduction of the line's 747s, and the labor and financial difficulties of 1969, he decided the company needed to make some changes, and first needed a close reading on employe attitudes. He ordered an extensive survey, and to show his personal interest in it, made a special film to be shown to all employes, asking them to respond to the questionnaire. "We need your active involvement in the company, in policy making, in making it go," he said. He asked for ideas on "how to make it a better place to work, a more productive, rewarding place, a fun place as well as a work place, if you will."

The survey covered a representative sampling of employes at all Pan Am locations with U.S. dollar payroll personnel. After the results had been tabulated, fifteen executives, each responsible for one phase of Pan Am operations, examined them to see what was causing trouble and where to make changes. Many innovations suggested by the survey were tried out even before the results were completely tabulated. Communications were found to be inadequate, so Halaby ordered a force of Pan Am executives out to talk with, and listen to, employes at every level, in small groups, at Pan Am stations around the U.S. and some foreign bases. They were assigned to gather employes' advice and hear their complaints, and to talk at all levels from cargo handler to station manager.

Among the changes made as a result of the survey and interviews was liberalization of employe travel policy, a new reward system for salesmen, a new booklet giving specifics on employe benefits, and a new twenty-five-year recognition program. In response to complaints about supervision, a training course for supervisors from top executives on down was introduced teaching them how to lead and to understand their workers. Other changes that may seem less important but that count mightily, such as modifications of stewardesses' uniforms, a better method of training baggage handlers, and changes in galleys to improve food service, were also suggested as a result of the program. Pan Am is aware that such survey programs often cause more talk than action, and the company's executives took pains to assure its personnel that it intended to follow through with the changes, not allow them to become one-shot, empty gestures.

Among the hardest jobs to improve are the telephone service positions that increasing numbers of companies have to fill, for reservations, complaints, orders, credit checks, and the like. American Airlines determined to enrich the jobs of its telephone reservation agents in Los Angeles, following the methods prescribed by AT&T's Robert Ford in his book *Motivation Through the Work Itself*. The jobs American chose for improvement are rigidly circumscribed, since the agents must wear headsets, must remain in front of the computer terminals, cannot leave the positions, and have no control over incoming calls. The calls are routed automatically, so the agent cannot build a personal relationship with customers. Despite this, reservationists are considered essentially as salespeople, and are expected to meet certain sales targets each day. American realized how limited the agents were in self-determination, but nevertheless believed it was possible to increase their participation in setting goals, developing more effective ways to do the job, and increasing the self-monitoring of their performance. Thus they would to a significant extent be instructing and supervising themselves. The real changes were not to be in the job itself, but in the way those doing the job were managed.

The supervisors worked up a list of fifty-one possible improvements, which was narrowed down to six changes. These were introduced with two groups of reservation agents, in an indirect fashion so the agents didn't know an experiment was under way. The changes were presented as "suggestions" by the supervisors at meetings with the agents. They emphasized self-evaluation and self-direction, with agents scoring themselves on their effectiveness with customers, calling back to correct any "bounces" (mistakes), and checking reservations on the Sabre computer system for accuracy. The supervisors also moved the reservation agents around to different jobs periodically, to relieve boredom and increase understanding of the overall functioning of the office. A review of the program after six months showed good productivity improvements, as measured by gross revenues generated, average revenue per eight-hour shift, and ratio of calls to sales. More important from the workers' point of view, perhaps, was the improvement in employe-management communications, and intangible improvements in job performance deriving from the self-evaluation procedures that were introduced. Mrs. Shirley Briggs, one of the reservation agents affected, says she likes the changes. She had found her job "terrifying" at first but now she feels "confident and competent." As a result of the changes that have been made, "there is a lot more variety in the work," she says, and she particularly likes the closer communication with her supervisor. She thinks the company's job-enrichment program "changed management's attitude, made supervisors aware of employes' needs." Now, she says, "I feel that he really cares about me, besides my job. He makes an effort to know everything that's going on. And if you've got an idea, he's interested."

In another effort to give some latitude to employes who are hemmed in on all sides by higher authority and standard procedures, American undertook to improve the morale, and the commitment, of sixteen of its employes at the Saint Louis airport who handle boarding of flights. They are called ramp ticket lift agents. Two agents were customarily assigned to each flight, under the direction of a supervisor. Under the new system, one of the agents was designated flight coordinator, and was made responsible for getting the flight into the air, without the need to clear any but the most unusual decisions with the supervisor. A survey taken after six months showed the agents felt significantly greater responsibility, and believed they had more opportunity to make worthwhile contributions. One flight coordinator delayed a takeoff to accommodate twenty passengers from a competing airline that had canceled its flight, judging that the additional revenues would justify the delay. He got the call five minutes before scheduled takeoff, held the flight until the twenty were aboard, without clearing with the supervisors—and was complimented for his decision. An agent summed up the job changes in an interview, saying, "I have more confidence in myself now that I see the confidence management has in me." The effort by American in Saint Louis illustrates that changes and improvements can be made in almost any sort of white-collar job. It also shows that, as is almost always the case, passing the authority down the line to lower levels gives the supervisors more time to do their real jobs, rather than spending their time second-guessing people on the scene who should have the authority to make decisions themselves.

Solutions for the malaise felt by engineers are more difficult to prescribe than for less painstakingly trained workers, because much of their problem is educational and psychological, and thus harder to remedy. Some far-seeing critics have for years been urging engineers to take their destiny more into their own hands, but this has not been easy. Dr. Simon Ramo, the vice-chairman of TRW, Inc., as long ago as 1962 called for what he designated "greater engineering," in proper mesh with social, industrial, economic, governmental, and psychological needs. Jay W. Forrester, the multifaceted MIT professor who developed the ferrite computer memory core, and wrote *Urban Dynamics* and other important system-analysis books, has publicly attacked the profession of engineering for submerging its ethics and integrity in the service of large organizations. Ralph Nader, who has spoken so much on so many subjects and has been vindicated so often, told a meeting of engineering educators in 1966 that a new concept of "remedial engineering" was needed, to reduce the "social costs of private enterprise and ameliorate the painful by-products of great engineering accomplishments." Engineers, he said, were too concerned with means, too indifferent to ends, and were glaringly absent from "public safety frontiers." More recently, he urged employed professionals to "blow the whistle" on their companies if the companies' activities harm the public interest. So there has been no shortage of warnings about the need for new approaches, both from within and from without the profession. But few engineers have responded.

The most logical place to attack the problem is in the engineering schools, where young engineers spend four or more of the most professionally significant years of their lives. Accordingly, it is on the engineering campuses that much of the important reform work is going on. There is probably no engineering school in the country that has not made extensive changes in its curriculum, in its pace of instruction, and in its course content over the past decade. A basic shift has been an effort to correct the overemphasis on theory that developed in the late 1950s and 1960s, and to restore a broader approach. Scientific knowledge grew so fast during that period, and became so complex, that what few humanities courses there were at many engineering schools were reduced to negligible importance. Now the trend is to teach students to see the whole effect of their work on human lives and on society, rather than breaking problems down to impersonal dehumanized components.

The movement toward broadening the scope of engineering training is seen at large, old schools, and at smaller, newer ones. At MIT the compendium of courses "relating to public policy or science and technology in society" grew from five pages in 1968 to thirty-seven pages in 1971, and includes courses such as the "Recycling of Materials," "Slums," and "Private Industry and Environmental Problems." At Oakland University's engineering school, in Rochester, Michigan, which started in 1965 and by 1971 had five hundred engineering students, Dean John E. Gibson seeks to increase student involvement by having them help set their own goals for courses and organize their laboratories. The school proposes to conduct interdisciplinary research linking engineering with medicine, ecology, and urban life.

Many engineering schools are attacking the problem of underutilization or deprofessionalization by offering new courses leading to technical degrees, like the two-year associate in technology, and the four-year bachelor of science in engineering technology. These courses will equip students to perform at the technical level, but for conceptual and design functions, further study will be required. With more technicians available, there will be less of a temptation to use engineers for work not requiring their full expertise.

Greater efforts are being made, too, to broaden the application of computers to engineering problems, so as to reduce the drudgery and free men's and women's minds for creative engineering. Professor Charles L. Miller, who has led MIT's effort to apply computers to engineering, says the computer is not merely a new tool, but offers "a new perspective on new ways of engineering." Computer languages for civil engineering, structural engineering, and other specialties have been developed that multiply the capabilities of men at middle and upper levels. Now, they can deal directly with the computer and get instant answers, rather than requesting data from junior engineers below them, and wasting time waiting for replies. The computer also allows engineers to take more factors into consideration, including

public sensitivities over matters such as highway locations, because the basic time-consuming work is speeded
up. Now, Miller says, engineers can offer alternative
solutions, instead of setting forth one uncompromising
recommendation, as used to be customary. This ability
to offer alternatives will help change the public image of
engineers from inflexible dictators of technology, and
ease some of the frictions between them and the communities in which they work. Eventually, it should help
improve their own image of themselves.

A serious shortcoming of engineering education in the
recent past has been a lack of rapport between the
schools and industry, which is in effect the customer for
the engineers trained at those schools. Industry executives have claimed that graduating engineers knew an
abundance of theory but couldn't perform any practical
engineering work. This was due to the heavy emphasis
placed on pure science in the curricula. A partial solution has been the co-op approach, under which students
alternate periods of study and work in industry. Now
more measures are being taken to bring campus and
plant closer. The Institute of Technology of Southern
Methodist University, under Dean Thomas L. Martin,
Jr., has a multi-pronged program for achieving this that
is proving highly successful. It is aimed both at keeping
engineering graduates up to date with technology, and
maintaining close links with the industries those engineers serve.

SMU broadcasts engineering courses over a micro-
wave circuit serving forty-two classrooms in thirteen
plants over a fifty-mile radius around Dallas, as a
member of a network formed by seven north Texas col-

leges and universities. Engineers at the plants see live TV broadcasts of actual courses as they are given in the SMU classroom-studios. The industrial students have direct telephone lines to the instructor so that they can ask questions during classes. They can take any of an array of courses leading to a master's degree, without ever setting foot on campus, or attending a single evening class. Examinations and papers are distributed and picked up by a daily courier service. The cost of $300 per course is in many cases paid by the student's company, in some cases by the student himself.

Dr. Martin also keeps his faculty in touch with industry by encouraging professors to serve as consultants with nearby companies. This keeps them up to date on practical problems graduating students will face. Engineers working in industry are in turn invited to serve at SMU as visiting professors, which further heightens the practicality of instruction. Martin has also organized a board of directors for the Institute that includes high officers of the firms participating in the graduate program, providing still another channel for gathering information on what business needs from its engineers. "We refuse to stay in an ivory tower," Martin says. "We feel our mission is to interact and cooperate with our industrial counterparts."

A major preoccupation at almost every engineering school is the need to instill into students a capacity for self-renewal. Engineering graduates have what is grimly known as a "half-life" of only five to ten years, depending on what branch of engineering they have studied. If they are not given the means of instructing themselves on a continuing and regular basis, they will fairly quickly become obsolete and useless both to their employers and to themselves.

Avoiding such obsolescence is one of the main concerns of the companies that depend on foresight and innovation from their engineering staffs for continued success in the marketplace. Honeywell, Inc., of Minneapolis, is helping work out a closed-circuit TV network with the University of Minnesota engineering school, like that in operation at SMU, to keep its engineers up to date, and also finances advanced courses taken by its engineers. The company provides "dual track" promotions for engineers who choose to remain in research or design rather than going over into management. The dual track concept offers pay and title grades for staff men comparable to those for line men, so that research-inclined engineers can feel they are moving up a career ladder and are not being overlooked by the company, or bypassed by the managers. Honeywell encourages its employes to involve themselves in public issues, even the hottest ones, and its high officers set the example: Vice-president Robert P. Henderson appeared with some blunt testimony at hearings in Washington on the threat to privacy posed by computer data banks— although Honeywell is a major manufacturer of computers.

John R. Dempsey, Honeywell's vice-president for science and engineering, says the company seeks to avoid fostering overspecialization, which leads to obsolescence and is limiting both for the company and for its employes, by encouraging the colleges with which it deals to give a broader education, with more humanities and communications courses, and more languages. New engineers are no longer put through a specified training program, but "start engineering right off," Dempsey says. "We find that a new man who has not specialized will often have new ideas for solving the problems we encounter."

The National Society of Professional Engineers works to enhance professional development and to get engineers involved in public affairs. It gives annual awards to organizations it judges have done the most to keep their engineers current on the state of their art. Through its chapters around the country, it sponsors an extensive series of public affairs involvement workshops, to make engineers aware of areas in which they can contribute to solving society's problems. Engineering students from local schools, as well as graduate practicing engineers, take part in these workshops.

The long-prevailing indifference of engineers to the social consequences of their work, which has brought them so much criticism, now is beginning to show signs of change. Some of the activist tactics used on campuses and by peace groups have been extended, rather tentatively, to engineering. At the 1971 annual convention in New York of one of the biggest specialized engineering societies, the Institute of Electrical and Electronic Engineers, which has 130,000 members, a dissident group called the Committee for Social Responsibility in Engineering picketed the main meeting and invited delegates to attend its own separate session. At the committee's New Engineering Conference, there were discussions of individual responsibility in engineering, the shortcomings of engineering organizations, and effects of government policies on engineers. Attendance at the sessions was small but the rebel engineers' and scientists' point was made, just as dissident young doctors made their point a year earlier when they invaded the American Medical Association convention to denounce its procedures. Students in engineering schools have also begun to demand that engineers scrutinize their assignments and refuse those not in keeping with ecological and social imperatives. At MIT, a group called ECIS, whose members disagree with many of the goals and methods of business, government, and universities, offers "participative action" seminars at which ECIS members present their point of view to business executives. They stress that this kind of communication is preferable to campus violence, and can help prevent such violence from occurring.

Another result of the discontent some engineers feel about their profession, especially about the insecurity that has afflicted some of them lately, is increased interest in unions. There are several dozen engineering unions around the country, most, like the Seattle Professional Engineering Employes Association, avoiding the term *union* and stressing the professional focus of the organization. A national federation called the Council of Engineers and Scientists Organizations (CESO) represents more than one hundred thousand unionized engineers, scientists, and technicians in the U.S. and Canada, and its program sums up what many of the union members want. CESO wants enrollments in engineering schools cut by 50 percent over the next five years, and wants limits placed on the number of alien engineers allowed to enter the United States. By holding down the supply of engineers, CESO evidently hopes to improve their bargaining position, somewhat as construction unions have been able to do for their members. A lot of engineers, however, oppose union membership, because they feel, or want to feel, that they are part of management rather than part of the work force. Many have moved up into engineering from union families, and don't want to slip back. They dislike the leveling effect of unions, and fear losing their voices among the large numbers of technicians and subprofessionals, classified as engineers, who dominate many of the engineering unions. Philosophically, union membership seems to many to represent the opposite direction from that they wish to pursue toward greater professionalism and more responsibility for their work and their own careers.

The main difference in the demands made by the new workers, particularly the younger workers, at differing levels from blue-collar to managerial and professional is not in their substance, but in their intensity. Young blue-collar workers out of high schools or trade schools, and young executive trainees out of business schools, with master's degrees, all want many of the same things from their jobs. But the young managers are more intransigent, because they have been exposed to the university climate where activism in the 1960s obtained many of the things students demanded. They also know they have something quite special to sell: their potential as leaders in the companies they serve. They are determined not to sell it out. Blue-collar workers, and increasingly, white-collar workers and even engineers, have the awful feeling that they can be replaced. They have little to offer that makes them special, and they have to tone down their complaints, particularly at times when unemployment is high. They also often lack the eloquence needed to express the *why* of their discontent. This goes far toward explaining why many blue-collar workers simply abstain from work, mutely registering their terrible dissatisfaction with it, while the young managers complain more openly, and when they are not given satisfaction, break abruptly by quitting and going off to seek fulfillment elsewhere.

The nature of their demands, for more responsibility and participation, and for corporate dedication to improving society and the environment, was set forth in an earlier chapter.

To meet requirements for immediate responsibility, a demand so widespread among junior managers that it is almost taken for granted, companies respond in different ways, sometimes through an organized program approach, sometimes less ritualistically. At Citizens and Southern National Bank, there is little emphasis on formal structure, but junior managers quickly find they are expected, and allowed, to think for themselves. Karen Hardy, twenty-seven, assistant advertising director, praises the bank's approach to junior managers. She says, "Around here they give you all the responsibility you can handle, and all the rope you need to hang yourself. It's very exciting." Pacific Telephone, with different kinds of problems, takes a different kind of approach. It operates a Management Achievement Program that puts decision pressure on the persons in it. Charles Wood, twenty-seven, an accounting supervisor who went through it, describes how he reacted. "In MAP," he said, "they give you responsibility right away, you learn as you go. I had responsibility in the military service, with seventy-five men under me, and I wanted a job with good gravity, one that was important to the company, with responsibility, with real work—not make work—a job in which I could learn as I went along."

A thirst for risk and challenge goes with the hunger for responsibility. William P. Moore, twenty-eight, went through a special General Electric Company program for high-potential recruits, and quickly moved up to handle the requirements for a major client of GE's information service division. He approves of the pressure. "It gives you more opportunity," he says. "It's not a safe job, you can't just put in eight hours a day. I prefer a job with high risk and the possibility of rapid advancement to taking a safe job."

The demand for early responsibility and the taste for risk implicitly carry with them the desire for rapid promotion, as Moore's remark makes clear. The goal often is not so much the money promotion brings, although that is not negligible, but the chance to have authority, a real voice in company decisions. Holiday Inns, in Memphis, Tennessee, has recognized the desire for autonomy among junior managers and, as the company has expanded, has left them a lot of freedom. John L. Baber, twenty-six, director of stockholder relations for the company, says that in his job he has "the freedom to make mistakes, an opportunity for responsibility without having to grab to get it. If you stifle people in my age group," he adds, "you're going to lose them."

The exacting set of dos and don'ts, and likes and dislikes, set forth by the junior managers confronts the corporations that need these men and women with some difficult problems. Top executives have to create movement of many sorts to attract and hold these highly mobile, demanding young employes. There must be job movement, so that they can acquire responsibility quickly. This means rapid promotions and unless the promotions are accomplished with surpassing finesse, they are likely to irritate older employes who see the younger persons being moved up over them. Such promotions, combined with the pressures of an until-recently rising job market, also cause severe salary compression. The man with three, four, or five years on the job sees a new employe with no experience getting a salary that nearly matches his, and is bound to be dismayed, if not embittered. A directly related problem is the inevitable slowing of job movement as the junior manager advances up to levels where promotions are less frequent. He feels that he is losing momentum, becomes worried and frustrated. Dr. William C. Byham, a management consultant, says he finds increasing realization in industry that after giving junior managers early responsibility, "the question becomes, What do you do after they are given this initial challenge? How do you follow the act?"

Movement is also required in a broader sense. The company must continue growing and diversifying so that it can offer opportunity to good people. This requirement is imposed at a time—the first time in American history—when growth has come into question as being possibly more harmful than helpful. The need to grow, but to grow without doing harm, constitutes a hazardous set of shoals for managements to negotiate.

One answer seems to be decentralization, breaking large corporations into smaller profit centers. Another is the creation of new ventures within the corporate structure, allowing young managers to explore new areas of endeavor and giving them full authority in areas they develop successfully.

Because of all these requirements, executives find in hiring junior managers that they have to concentrate increasingly on selling their company, rather than waiting to be sold by the applicant on his or her virtues. Similarly, companies have to commit themselves on contentious issues, and do formerly unheard-of things such as giving employes paid time off on a regular basis for community or social work, if they wish to attract concerned activists who often have the greatest promise for the company's future.

Executives also are learning that they have to pay much closer attention to the training of the men who train new junior managers coming into the company. Edgar H. Schein, of MIT's Alfred Sloan School of Management, has studied closely the disaffection of junior managers in their first jobs and found that the influence of the new employe's first boss can be crucial. "It is the first boss who can launch the graduate into a successful career or into corporate oblivion," Schein says. He finds it paradoxical that while many companies have elaborate training programs for incoming college graduates, few train the men who determine how the graduate is utilized after he begins work.

Linked with this requirement is the need to follow up on the new employes and pay close attention to their continuing development. James A. Henderson, operations vice-president of Cummins Engine Company, of Columbus, Indiana, says, "The old way of bringing people in at the bottom and hoping the cream will rise doesn't work. You have to handcraft jobs for them, put them under a good manager, and watch carefully so the older people don't kill them off."

Corporations also have to work out new relations with colleges and universities in order to fill the need for continuing learning that will be required as jobs become more complex and change more rapidly. That relationship will become more flexible. The "box" concept of education, with sixteen to twenty years of straight schooling that comes to an abrupt and final end, will be modified to a "slope line" concept, with internships, summer jobs in industry, and work experience interspersed with more education, and continuing education after graduation. More corporations will operate their own advanced training centers, and they will cooperate closely with universities. In another aspect of campus relations, corporations will increasingly find themselves obliged to justify their procedures and positions to campus groups such as Stanford's Committee for Corporate Responsibility and other chapters of this organization across the country. This will mean closer and more frequent contact between managers and students, and should result in better understanding.

Many of the concerns expressed by young managers center around the extent to which they are treated as individuals, their abilities are used, their ideas are listened to. Harry Levinson, the author and psychologist, formerly of the Menninger Foundation and more recently a visiting professor at the Harvard Business School, explains the need for personal recognition. "People need attachments for growth," he says, "and they attach themselves to people, to objects, to houses, and to organizations. They *want* to latch on to companies, *if* they can be effective, do a good job of work, solve problems, and look good to themselves." The fundamental point, he says, is that "all successful industrial organizations are re-creations of the family."

Levi Strauss and Company, in San Francisco, exemplifies the family image—it was privately held from its founding in 1850 and only went public in 1971. Thomas Kasten, a product manager at Levi Strauss, says of the family feeling at the company: "I noticed it when I came here. Every once in a while I would run into the president, Walter Haas, Jr., in the hall, and he says hello to me by name. Levi Strauss is very people oriented." This means that, among other things, the organization is wide open to suggestions. "If you have an idea outside your area, you are free to walk in to see the manager of another department. If it's a good idea, he's going to listen to you." Kasten contrasts the feeling at Levi Strauss with the experience of friends of his who work elsewhere and complain that "they are just another number, just another resource, like steel for fabrication."

Along with this yearning for individual recognition and for belonging, junior managers want stimulating colleagues from whom they can learn and with whom they can exchange ideas. Alert companies try to make sure they get the kind of colleagues they want. David Moffett, twenty-eight, an investment manager with Kaiser Aluminum and Chemical Corporation, in Oakland, California, looked around carefully after getting his MBA degree from Berkeley. "I interviewed with a railroad company," he says. "They were all a bunch of guys with little railroad things on their ties. You were bound to think that if you stuck there you would have a helluva job if you were patient, because everybody around is a bunch of clods. While here at Kaiser, you have guys that are really fabulous, so the competition is a little tougher. But it's a lot more stimulating atmosphere."

Many of the junior managers who share these goals conclude that a small company, or a small division of a larger corporation, offers the best opportunity for gaining the responsibility and individuality they seek. Groups of students in recent classes at both the Harvard and Stanford business schools have raised funds to advertise their preference for working for small companies. They believe small firms not only offer more responsibility earlier but allow the individual more control over his life.

The Cummins Engine Company is one of the three hundred largest corporations in the country, but its executives are aware of the advantages of smallness and make studied efforts to preserve a human scale. In planning a large new plant that was to be completed in 1972, Cummins's management determined to make the factory seem a collection of small units, rather than one vast impersonal building in which men and women would feel lost. This feeling for scale is appreciated by its junior managers, as John Laemmer, thirty, explains in comparing Cummins with the Air Force, in which he spent two years and which he describes as "stagnant." He says, "The international division has a small company atmosphere. There are fewer people to do the jobs." As a result, and because Cummins was increasing its commitments overseas, "you got total responsibility. You have to be given the opportunity to fail in order to grow."

In a broad sense, what the young managers hope for in their jobs is a freewheeling, unstructured setting analagous to what they sought—and largely obtained—a few short years ago on their campuses. For this reason, the junior manager training programs that prove most appealing to the trainees are those with the least formal structure and the greatest degree of flexibility. Many companies trying to make improvements in this area have abandoned the term *trainee* altogether, and some have abolished all vestiges of a formal program, moving new men into specific jobs after a day or so of familiarization with the company. Clyde R. Claus, vice-president of Marine Midland Bank, who is responsible for recruiting and executive development, says of the unstructured program, "We used to 'butterfly them, from one department to another. Now it's like marriage—when they're ready." At Marine Midland and other forerunner companies, the old thirty-six-month rotational approach, under which the new employe methodically spent a set number of weeks in one department after another, watching check-canceling machines or adding subtotals to check ledgers, is out.

The junior managers also want a voice in setting the organization's goals, something not many would have even thought of demanding as recently as five years ago. Arjay Miller, former president of the Ford Motor Company, and now dean of the Stanford graduate business school, says, "The young executive is going to have to be a party to the decision-making process. This is dignity. This is part of the life-style. It is the kind of change organizations of the future must make in order to operate in the new environment, in this new participatory democracy." Bearing this out, Lawrence R. Knowles, general manager of Memorex's business products division, who has worked for Xerox and Kaiser and who has hired many junior managers although he himself is only in his early thirties, says business graduates coming out of school now are "noticeably different even than those of my generation." He explains, "They are better informed. They've developed a more questioning attitude. They won't accept the status quo and they won't accept irrational behavior on the part of management. They have a greater concern for the long-range implications of company policies; they care more about this than about watching quarter-by-quarter results. It's more important for them to really be involved in setting goals. If they don't have a say in setting them, and don't agree they are correct, there is less commitment."

The new demands junior managers make of their employers for corporate social concern and effectiveness are less than universal requirements so far, but they are potentially of equal, if not greater, importance than the job-related requirements. It is the forerunners, those who set the pace for their contemporaries, who are calling for a social conscience on the part of the corporations. Enlightened managers of some farsighted companies have already committed their firms to the pursuit of social goals, not just to attract able junior managers but because they believe it is their obligation to do so. Those companies that have not taken a position on the matter

will find it increasingly difficult to enlist the most talent-
ed management candidates, and will experience growing internal pressure from those already aboard. Ernest
C. Arbuckle, whose position as chairman of the Wells
Fargo Bank and former dean of the Stanford Business
School, at the crossroads of education and industry, affords him unique insight into the junior manager's
mind, has spoken publicly and vigorously on the subject.

Arbuckle says, "Business exists in and for society. . . .
the corporation does have a responsibility to society
beyond the maximization of profit." In some cases, he
judges, "profitability will have to be measured in the
long term and in a more general sense than has been
traditional." The Wells Fargo Bank, eleventh largest in
the U.S., has an impressive record, in keeping with Arbuckle's words, of giving jobs, business loans, and training to minority persons. It also makes many student
loans, has established an urban affairs department, and
is contributing to nature conservancy.

In search of specific guidance on the youthful point of
view, Arbuckle and Wells Fargo President Richard Cooley hired a Stanford graduate student in the fall of 1970
to study the bank's participation in the solution of social
problems, and to make recommendations. The student,
Kirk Hanson, then twenty-four, already had some expertise in this new field, having worked during the summer
of 1967 with Hewlett-Packard, in Palo Alto, California,
as one of the nation's first "radicals in residence," to
convey the viewpoint of young people to management.
He is currently head of the National Affiliation of Concerned Business Students.

The question of social responsibility is closely tied in

with the making and allocating of profits in business. Junior managers who have emerged from college in the last few years increasingly question the validity of profit for profit's sake alone. This was one of the central findings of a major study done by Daniel Yankelovich, Inc., for John D. Rockefeller III, on youth attitudes, in which hundreds of college students and executives were surveyed. The study showed that the number of students believing profit is too central a concern of business rose from 53 percent in 1969, to 67 percent in 1970, an increase of 14 percent in just one year. The trend is also shown by the high level of interest in Stanford's Committee for Corporate Responsibility, which after only one year included 20 percent of the graduate school students.

However, those who are willing to go into business at all, rather than shunning it for social service or government work, accept the fundamental necessity of profits. They understand economics and realize that profits are necessary to attract investors, and to finance the creation of new opportunity. But they accept profits only if they are for good ends, and are achieved without misrepresentation or exploitation.

The Maxwell House Division of General Foods Corporation, in a farsighted effort to establish communication, brought twelve of its junior managers together for three days at a special session to discuss shortcomings they perceived in their jobs. In their report prepared for the division president, one of the three principal headings was: "Are Profits Enough?" The young managers said there was a universal feeling that the company was not doing enough in social involvement, in enriching the lives of its employes, in ecological and antipollution activity, but was concentrating unduly on profits. The delegates did not criticize profits as such, but questioned their allocation, contending that the division should in effect put more of what it took *out* of the economy *back* in ways that will improve society. This kind of effort, bringing together outspoken employes and soliciting their views on corporate policies, can backfire if it is mishandled or if it is done just as window dressing. But when it is properly carried out, it has a double usefulness. It brings frank criticism of the company policies to the attention of top management while the criticism is still nascent and while there is time to take corrective action. And it shows the concerned employes that management genuinely wants to know what is on their minds, which goes a long way toward defusing anger over policies with which they disagree.

The mounting strength and urgency of the demands on corporations to involve themselves in society's problems was reflected in conversations and interviews with junior managers in every section of the country. John Baber, the stockholder relations director for Holiday Inns, says, "Before I went to work here I did some checking around to see what the minority hiring picture was and whether there was equal opportunity. I was satisfied, and I still am." He plans to use his legal training to try some cases for the American Civil Liberties Union, and is confident that "there won't be any objection" to this from the company.

At National Airlines in Miami, Stephen Kilski, twenty-nine, an industrial relations staff representative, says it is important to him that he can work on social problems with company approval and support. Admitting National once had a reputation for discrimination, he says, "We have been working very hard trying to change things and I think it's improving every day." Thomas Kasten, the product manager at Levi Strauss, put the social-involvement requirement even more directly. "The company firmly believes in the social responsibility of business—that to be a good business citizen you have to be a good citizen in general. I couldn't work for a company that didn't have this policy and belief. By working for Levi, I can work for a company without having to sacrifice any of my own social consciousness."

It is not possible to predict to what extent economic reverses may deflect the reforming instincts of the junior managers, but it seems doubtful that any fluctuations in the economy can permanently obviate them. These are profound, subterranean movements, not surface ripples or eddies. If business fails to respond and the confrontation becomes more harsh, there may be truly grave developments. George Koch, president of the Grocery Manufacturers' Association, has already predicted that within five years a group of junior managers will "lock a president of a major corporation out of his office" to force concessions from the company. Because things always seem to happen faster in this country than anyone dares predict, the first such lockout may come in months, not years.

Taking the view of the most gloomy prophets, the angry attitude of youth could infect older persons above them, and work downward in the ranks to production workers, resulting in a massive industrial mutiny. Loyalty to the company will decline further as junior managers conclude the company is not loyal to them, and as ever more frequent moves make each job a transient affair. The counter-culture will grow and offer a readily available alternative to corporate employment, with increasing numbers of boutiques, communes, and craft shops. Many will drop out of the system as a political protest against goals with which they disagree. The possessions the young are taught to covet will intrigue them less and less. The most able students will be the least willing to take corporate jobs, leaving only the less imaginative, less gifted persons available.

This is, to repeat, the view of gloomy prophets. Fortunately, more and more farsighted executives are coming to understand the changes that are going on, and are taking measures to forestall such a breakdown. Significantly, there appears to be a continuum of concern and awareness in the companies run by these men. The same firm that is striving to improve the jobs of its production and white-collar workers, and junior managers and executives, is often the firm that is doing the most in social areas such as minority employment, pollution abatement, and consumer problems. General Foods is not only convening its junior managers to discuss company policy with top executives, it is striving to increase its minority work force, investing in research on biodegradable packaging materials, researching ways to improve the nutrition value of its products. The Wells Fargo Bank hires a consultant to advise management on social and youth concerns; it also makes low-cost housing loans, trains hard-core workers, helps finance ghetto enterprises. Pacific Telephone, with its unusual utility-monopoly position, strives to expand and improve service to consumers, while reaffirming its commitment to the cities, to increased minority hiring, and to bettering jobs at every level in the company. Levi Strauss takes a national lead in fighting racism, refusing to build plants where discrimination is accepted as local policy—and works to enhance its jobs. There are other examples of this sort of broad concern, but there are far more examples of companies that are taking no positive steps and that do not even seem aware that there is a need to make improvements.

It becomes clear, in examining the positive-change companies as compared to the no-change companies, that the fundamental motive force bringing improvements almost invariably comes from the top management. Only when the highest executives endorse job improvements and social involvement do their subordinates feel able, or willing, to take the necessary procedural steps. Put another way, there's not much the men at the lower level can do if they don't have the backing and overt support of their chief executives. J. Irwin Miller, chairman of the Cummins Engine Company, exemplifies the kind of granite determination to improve jobs and lives and the community that, when evident at the very top, can permeate every level of a company. Miller is famous for his multiple contributions to Columbus, and to the country. He has served on federal commissions, university and foundation boards, religious groups, has enriched Columbus with work by America's finest architects, and funded a variety of civic projects and activities. All this while building Cummins into the country's largest producer of Diesel engines for highway use. Miller has understood the twin needs of improving jobs and meeting social obligations that, taken together, sum up the requirements of the bright young junior managers.

Miller's actions and those of his company are the most eloquent testimonial to his convictions concerning corporate responsibility. Cummins is conducting research to reduce pollutant emissions from its engines. It supports minority enterprises around the country with subcontracting agreements and technical counsel. It works out new management development programs giving more responsibility earlier. It actively seeks out and trains minority group employes at every level. It takes an active role in community affairs, contributing abundant corporate executive time and attention toward the solution of national problems, especially the time of Miller himself, who has served hundreds and hundreds of hours over many years on public boards and commissions.

But while the company's actions speak most loudly for Cummins's viewpoint, Miller has eloquent words on these concerns, too. Industry, he believes, has until now paid more attention to its machines than to its people. "We have been late accommodating people. We have to pay serious, dignified attention to individuals. We will stand or fall on how we handle this." This will mean, among other things, an end to firing people to meet passing economic difficulties. "We've reached the point," Miller says, "when we can't fight inflation by firing those least able to defend themselves." As for the specific needs of younger employes, Miller says, "the ethic of the young is to contribute. The best way to keep the ablest of the young people is to load them up a little beyond their capacity. That capacity then turns out to be very high."

He criticizes the veneration of age for age's sake alone: "The factor to consider is people's competence, the extent to which they are looking ahead. Older people may just be bringing experience from a world that no longer exists." Miller has practiced what he preaches: in 1969 the Cummins board of directors elected a group of men whose average age was under forty as the active operating management of the company. "There are times," Miller says, "when you have dramatic changes in society and business, when past explicit experience is of less use."

Miller speaks for the highest ideals of American enterprise, and expresses the kind of viewpoint younger employes are hungry to hear, when he appraises the role and the responsibility of the corporation. "Every business," he says, "is the beneficiary, for free, of services such as schools and government, and of enriching elements such as art and religion, which it did not pay for and without which it could not exist. The only way the businessman *can* pay for them is to work to make sure the community will continue—to work for good schools, and parks, for churches that care. There is no such thing as a free lunch."

The motive for taking this responsibility, he says, derives from the American tradition. "You don't behave right because it pays, but because it's right, just as you try to build a good engine. There's no faster way to go broke than to seek to make a profit."

The success of business, and by extension of the society within which and for which it functions, will depend, he says, on the extent to which we "welcome and accept change. An awful lot of people in our society now feel very threatened by change. This will be the second American revolution, and it will be as painful as anything we've ever seen. It will mean enormous cost; it will mean lowering our private, individual standard of living to raise our public standard of living; it will mean changing our public institutions to accommodate continuing change." In his sixties, and a hundred times a millionaire, he obviously does not make his pronouncements on youth and corporate obligations to serve either his generation or his financial interest, but, as he would say, because it's right.

The words of Irwin Miller represent a dizzying evolution from the philosophy of the robber barons. These are words of the future, words the young will want to hear and see acted upon, before they will engage themselves wholeheartedly in the difficult enterprises lying ahead that will require their efforts and their minds. The principles Miller enunciates will go far toward smoothing the difficult transition between old laissez-faire capitalism that built this country but minimized people and destroyed resources, and the new socially oriented, people-concerned corporation that will increasingly become the model of the 1970s.

# chapter

# *New Attitudes about People*

As workers become more demanding, managers are necessarily going to pay closer attention to their requirements and seek new ways of evaluating their contributions. Where employes were often taken for granted in the past, it is now becoming apparent to more and more executives that this attitude is no longer valid. Workers today enjoy a degree of personal and economic freedom they have never before known. Managers are going to have to pay more attention to the investment made in finding workers, hiring them, training them, developing them. They are going to have to become more aware of the costs of losing them, whether by day-at-a-time absenteeism of the sort suffered by the auto plants, or by high turnover, as occurred with some telephone company jobs, and as happens with junior managers who find they dislike their jobs or their companies. New methods for measuring the worth of workers, and for predicting their performance, are going to become more important. Some of them are already in use, and others are on the way.

An innovation of considerable potential importance, which forces managers to think of employes in a totally different way, has been put into use in one American company, and is being examined by several others here and in Canada and Japan. It is called human resources accounting. The concept was developed by William C. Pyle, who works with the University of Michigan's Institute for Social Research, of which Dr. Rensis Likert, who now heads his own consulting firm, was until recently director. Pyle defines human resource accounting as a method for evaluating an organization's investment in the development of an effective work force. It is not, he emphasizes, an attempt to place a dollar value on individual employes. The use of the word *accounting*, he says, "raises certain value issues that frankly turn off some people." HRA does not attempt to put values on human beings. What it does do is provide new information to supplement data managers use for guidance in making decisions.

Pyle says, "Our studies indicate that organizations frequently underestimate the magnitude of their investment in an effective work force. For one thing, the better part of a year's time may be consumed in breaking in a new manager or developing a new organization. During this familiarization period, more mistakes are made and normal responsibilities are frequently neglected. These 'hidden' costs are often substantial. Because the magnitude of this investment is typically underestimated, human assets are often written off too quickly. We can be certain that this has occurred in many firms which have cut back their personnel force during the 1970 recession." Furthermore, he says, new investments in developing people, through additional training, or travel, or attending conferences, are often cut at a time of recession. "What we are finding, however, is that knowledge of investments in employes changes the timing and magnitude of these decisions."

The human resources accounting method was first applied in 1968 at the R. G. Barry Corporation, a Columbus, Ohio, company that manufactures leisure wear. Initially the concept was applied only to managerial personnel, but later with time and experience, it was extended to cover the entire work force. The company included a pro forma statement on its human resources in its 1969 annual report. This was the first published industrial financial statement to include this information. The human resources data were contrasted with the conventional financial statements in a special section of the report. They showed net investments in managerial personnel of $986,000. (On an individual basis, the company invests approximately $3,000 in a first line supervisor, $15,000 in a middle manager, and upwards of $30,000 in hiring, familiarizing, and developing a top level executive.) The liabilities and stockholders' equity side of the balance sheet showed $493,000 for "Deferred Federal Income Taxes as a Result of Appropriation for Human Resources," and an equal amount under retained earnings for an "Appropriation for Human Resources."

On the income statement, a net change of $173,569 in human resource investments during 1969 was applied as a positive adjustment to income before taxes. After taxes, this change resulted in an upward adjustment of about $87,000 to conventionally determined net income of about $700,000. The adjustment reflected the fact that during 1969 new investments in human resources were undertaken more rapidly than they were written, as Pyle explains it in an article in the University of Michigan's *Michigan Business Review*. The figures brought an entirely new dimension to the annual report and had a significant effect on executive decision making, as is indicated by their remarks quoted below.

In 1969, Barry executives also prepared a "Human Resources Budget 1970," believed to be industry's first capital budget for human resources. It listed "new investments: management personnel; additions, replacements, development [and] transfer in," and showed hourly personnel separately, with a total figure under the new investment heading of $932,000 for the twelve-month plan. Under "write-offs," in the management personnel category, amortization for the twelve-month plan was carried at $138,000, turnover losses were broken down to voluntary and involuntary, running $80,000 and $60,000 respectively, and skill obsolescence was carried at $5,000. Under the hourly personnel category, write-offs were listed at $480,000. With a beginning balance of $1,325,000 and an ending balance of $1,383,000, the report showed a net change of $58,000. The report also showed the actual number of people involved in each category. With these figures in front of them, Barry executives can make more effective use of their human

resources, and can better appraise new business opportunities, because they can project the capital spending
required for personnel right along with the capital investment needed for physical plant and equipment. The
project has thus allowed executives of the corporation to
evaluate the company's investment in human resources
and determine the rate at which they should be amor-
tized. Having this information influences a variety of
corporate decisions. Armed with it, a manager is better
equipped to decide, for example, whether to close down
a slow-selling line and risk losing skilled employes and
the company's investment in them, or to sell the production below cost but retain the workers. Barry executives
emphasize that human resource accounting is not an end
in itself, but they say it is necessary to know one's
human resource investments, maintenance costs, and re-
turns in order to make valid decisions and plan long-
range corporate growth. Comments by Barry officials
illustrate how they use HRA and what they believe it
does for them.

Gordon Zacks, the company's president, says, "One
major objective for developing human resource accounting at the R. G. Barry Corporation is to improve our
measures of the over-all performance of decentralized
profit centers and cost centers. This need becomes increasingly important as our organization becomes larger.
We were concerned that a division might, for example,
report unrealistic profits through liquidation of un-
measured human assets."

Barry's vice-president for human resources, Robert L.
Woodruff, Jr., explains the application of HRA in actual
decision-making in a situation the company faced in

1970. "The 1970 recession required a downward adjustment in our personnel force. At the executive level, our preliminary analysis indicated that a number of highly capable people would have to be furloughed in order to meet our minimum profit plan. A more detailed analysis employing human resources accounting information indicated that too many employes would be laid off based on the conventional analysis. For example, a termination notice given one manager was rescinded after further study indicated that substantial investments were required over a two- to three-year period to bring him up to the expected level of proficiency. We determined that the write-off would not be in the firm's interest since we were confronted with a short-term recession rather than a long-term retrenchment. We did not drastically curtail our internal and external personnel development activities as we might have done based upon the conventional analysis. In fact, we created and filled new positions in our organization to support long-term profit objectives."

Looking at the situation from the financial specialist's perspective, Edward Stan, Barry's treasurer, says, "Our industry is subject to seasonal fluctuation and we have to periodically adjust our work force in relation to sales volume. If production exceeds sales, we incur additional costs of carrying the excess inventory. On the other hand, when we reduce the work force, investments in human resources must be written off. In addition we know that new investments will have to be made in hiring replacements when sales pick up again. Analysis of human resource write-off and replacement cost data usually indicate that it is more advantageous for the company to build inventory for a longer period than the conventional analyses would indicate. Of course, if the business slump is protracted, layoffs do become necessary when the costs of carrying additional inventory exceed human resource write-offs and anticipated replacement costs." Here, Stan describes a fundamental change in attitude toward the work force that HRA has caused.

"Our knowledge of what is invested in our employes has increased our motivation to maintain and enhance that investment. For this reason we have tried to balance our production schedules over the entire year."

As the concept of human resource accounting is developed and becomes more familiar to executives, there will be more changes in thinking, more attention paid to the individuals who make up the work force of every organization. One measure of the eventual impact this may have is given by the reactions to a question Dr. Likert likes to ask chief executives. What, he asks, would be the probable cost of replacing their entire labor force, if they lost every employe and executive and had to start over with just their physical plant and equipment? The executives have been accustomed to placing values on plant and equipment, calculating the rates at which they can be written off, but many have never considered the worth of their employes to the company. After some moments of shocked, and often revealing, contemplation, and after emphasizing that no one really knows, the executives end up estimating the cost would probably be at least double their annual payrolls, some ranging as high as ten times payroll. Most estimate around three to five times.

An attempt to answer the same question was made by

Likert and Pyle in an article for the *Financial Analysts Journal*. They reckoned that the cost of rebuilding the entire human organization from scratch to its present level of effectiveness for a hypothetical company with a payroll of $500 million could range anywhere from $1.5 to $2.5 billion. Or, if the calculation is based on a firm's earnings, the company's human organization could be worth about twenty-four times earnings.

Likert and Pyle say, "Reports of current earnings of corporations are often unintentionally incorrect because sizable fluctuations in a substantial proportion of their total assets are now ignored by the accounting reports. Since a large proportion of corporate assets is neglected, the effect of management actions such as cost reduction programs is often unknown. Thus, for example, a 10 percent across the board cut in personnel may be reported as increasing earnings. The increase in cash flow from such cost reduction efforts is not necessarily earnings, however, since the cost reduction program usually has liquidated assets with value to the firm substantially in excess of the reported increase in 'earnings.' "

They conclude by pointing out that accurate accounting of human resources in financial reporting can be of crucial importance in evaluating a proposed merger, for example. "Costly mistakes are often made when acquisitions or mergers occur. The firm to be acquired or merged can create a highly misleading picture of the value of assets other than the physical and financial. The company can create this picture, for example, by selling low-cost, shoddy merchandise which yields high current earnings but liquidates customer loyalty. Similarly, spuriously high earnings can be achieved over a few years by punitive, high-pressure treatment of labor. The ruthless pressure for increased earnings will cause the most able personnel in the firm to seek and accept offers from other companies, and weaken labor's commitment to the organization and willingness to make cooperative efforts to achieve organization objectives."

Pyle and Likert emphasize that human resources accounting is still in an early stage, and that its full implications and benefits are yet to be realized. Within a few years, however, Likert says, "we expect to have procedures available to enable a firm to make reasonably accurate estimates of the trends occurring in the productive capabilities of its human assets. Financial reports will then reflect with reasonable accuracy the present financial state of an organization and changes in its financial condition through time and not ignore, as at present, serious fluctuations in one-third to one-half of its assets. These more accurate financial reports will also indicate the financial consequences of changes in causal variables such as leadership style, and intervening variables such as employe loyalties, attitudes, perceptions and motivations."

The change this approach will bring about in the way managers regard their workers will coincide neatly with the way workers increasingly expect to be regarded: as valuable, individual beings with their own characteristics and their own unique abilities. Managers who now tend to look more fondly on a new drill press or a high-speed computer than they do at the men and women who run them will be forced to take account of the worth of those people. This should bring more esteem for those workers. It should also result in a greater proclivity on management's part to let them improvise and initiate, to let them work to their fullest capacity and employ all

their abilities, latent as well as known ones. Human resources accounting could, in short, cause a striking difference in attitudes both of employed and of employers.

Another personnel innovation that has recently become quite popular is the use of assessment centers in
selecting employes for promotion. Assessment has
always been practiced in one form or another, whether
in simple interviews, in testing, in examining records of
candidates, or just by observation. The new wrinkle
here, and it goes back a few years now, is putting the
evaluation into a formal, ritualized situation, with
higher-ranking company officers who have never before
met the subject doing the assessment on the basis of
specified criteria. The method was developed during
World War II by the Office of Strategic Services (OSS)
to select agents. It was adopted in 1956 by AT&T, which
has continued its use and now has voluminous records
covering the results over more than fifteen years. AT&T
and affiliate companies test ten thousand persons each
year at fifty centers. By 1970 some forty companies were
using the technique, and it was spreading rapidly.

Different companies have differing methods, but the
usual approach is to bring eight to twelve persons to an
assessment center for three to four days. Generally they
are chosen because of good performance in their jobs as
technicians, and the aim is to select those who have the
potential to be promoted to management from the
ranks. Some companies are also sending middle managers to assessment centers. They spend their time at the
assessment center doing various exercises that simulate

management tasks and that allow measurement of the individuals' abilities in analysis and leadership, and rating of their behavior under pressure. There are the well-known "in-basket" problems, the challenging telephone calls from simulated superiors or customers, the thorny interviews with disgruntled employes, all of which are observed by assessors from senior management. Some candidates show executive flair, some falter during the exercise, realizing that the stress of executive life is not for them.

After the candidate leaves, the assessors prepare preliminary reports, then discuss each candidate individually, the discussions lasting up to one or two hours for each person. Out of this comes a rating indicating whether the candidate should remain in his present job, has limited, average, or above average potential, or has the stuff to reach top levels in the company—vice-president or president. The candidates are generally informed on how they did. Where they are given a choice of being told or not, most ask to be informed.

There are some potential hazards involved with assessment techniques. One of the obvious ones is the familiar exam syndrome—the guy who freezes up for his final exams and does badly; he may be superb in day-to-day decision-making but lack test-taking ability. Another is the negative effect of *not* being chosen for assessment center attendance. The men who are passed over know that certain of their colleagues have been chosen for evaluation and possible promotion, while they who are passed over are stuck at their present level. This can be dismissed as of no more importance than the normal disappointment felt when one is left behind as a contemporary is promoted. It seems quite different, however, because companies that use assessment centers often check out a wide gamut of employes, and a person who is not included but who has some ambition is bound to feel he is really out of it.

Still another problem is that of the man who goes through the assessment process and learns he does not meet the requirements. He may take it well, concluding that management is not for him and returning to his job, content with what he has and relieved at avoiding what would have been a situation of considerable stress. But he may also decide to look for a job at another company, where he might be more appreciated, and where he would not have the negative assessment center report on his record for anyone to see in considering promotions or new assignments. If he were driven away in this fashion, it would mean losing a man who must have been fairly good at what he was doing, or he wouldn't have been chosen for assessment. Or the man could decide to stay on in his job, but with a heavy heart and a leaden hand, disgruntled and negative for the rest of his career.

Dr. William C. Byham, a consultant who has been a leader in introducing assessment, says there are advantages beyond the obvious ones of systematizing the selection of future managers. Assessment centers, he says, "help young people in a company, because at the assessment center they are exposed to high-level management people. This is one of the great benefits. I've seen people skip levels and go right up after this kind of exposure." The centers also provide a setting for cross-fertilization between different plants in a company, because they bring candidates and assessors in from different areas.

Byham finds that a majority of persons assessed are in favor of the procedure, because it seems fair—fairer than being judged by just one boss—and it provides the assurance that one will not get lost in a huge company. In addition, he says, "it offers a fantastic chance to learn about oneself."

Part of the assessment technique's appeal, and part of its danger, is the promise of putting numerical or letter ratings on the potential of as yet untested candidates for management jobs. It is comforting to some managers to be able to cite test results as the basis for their judgments on promotability, rather than having to rely on their judgment of people as people. But this mechanistic, and sometimes arbitrary, quality seems to put formalized assessment at odds with the currents influencing today's younger workers, at whatever level. They are products of a more open society, which accepts people for what they are and what they do, and rejects arbitrary ratings, whether they are grades, or IQ test results. Granted, these young dissenters may be mistaken in rejecting such measurements, but in the current climate, putting a stamp on an employe's record—and metaphorically on his or her forehead—that will probably forever influence that employe's promotion possibilities in the company seems out of keeping with the times. It is convenient and practical, but it seems inhumane and insensitive to some observers.

It is quite obvious from the enthusiastic support given the assessment center concept by companies such as AT&T, J. C. Penney, IBM, Standard Oil (Ohio), and others that the advantages of the technique seem to easily outweigh any possible disadvantages. But whether the new generation of workers will accept being processed and graded in this way as acquiescently as did the older persons who have gone through it is uncertain. These new workers and junior managers didn't even accept the idea of grades in college. They won't want to be graded in life. Formalized assessment as presently practiced is quite foreign to the concept many of these younger workers have of themselves, and seems quite foreign to the way they intend to lead their lives.

# chapter

# 8

# *Work and Future Workers*

If change follows the pattern it has itself established, a pattern of acceleration and intensification, with new changes building on earlier ones and the net rate of change picking up speed, the quality of jobs is going to need a great deal more attention than it has been getting. If we pause to consider the future for a few moments, and project the trends already evident in the world of work, it will become apparent that in the not-too-distant future, hardly anyone will be willing to do jobs that are not reasonably attractive. Already, employers have difficulty getting people for certain kinds of undesirable jobs, and pay rates for those jobs have soared, even while desperate measures are being taken to improve such jobs so that they can be filled.

The increasing unwillingness to take such jobs will

derive both from the unattractive nature of the work it-self, or the conditions surrounding it, and from the ease with which unemployed persons will be able to survive. Many ghetto youths even now prefer to remain unem-ployed rather than take jobs they feel are degrading or are simply dead-end jobs. This trend too will intensify, if present conditions are a guide to the future.

There are those who argue against the need to im-prove jobs, some of them union officials who see the em-phasis on job enrichment and improving motivation as a threat to union power, some of them managers who "came up the hard way" and resent the new solicitude for employes. The viewpoint expressed by Frank Pol-lara, assistant research director for the AFL-CIO, at a conference at the University of North Carolina at Greensboro in February 1971, exemplifies how some un-ionists feel. Pollara told the conference, which dealt with motivation and industrial democracy, ". . . motivation, as I understand it, is an abstract concept that has very little relevance, very little pertinence, very little mean-ing for the industrial world today. . . . over the years there has developed a considerable body of literature on the subject. A good deal of it masquerades as scientific research, though probably better characterized as pseu-doscientific research. Most of it is unadulterated non-sense that has very little meaning in the real manage-ment-labor relationship field."

Presumably that "real management-labor relationship field" has nothing to do with creating good jobs and having them well done, increasing productivity and sat-isfactions on both sides, but is rather the adversary rela-tionship cultivated by some unions whereby labor is eternally pitted against management as its hostile rival. Or Pollara may resent efforts to develop motivation because they often succeed, and when they succeed in nonunion plants, they make it more difficult, if not impossible, for unions to organize those plants.

Pollara is certainly entitled to his opinion, and in view of the nature of his job, he should know what he is talking about. But a lot of studies, confirmed by interviews and by random observations around the country, indicate that he is mistaken. The level of concern over worker discontent, known to social scientists as alienation and to other more outspoken observers as job hatred, is increasing in corporations and in government circles. The Department of Labor's Jerome M. Rosow, assistant secretary of labor for policy, evaluation, and research, has made analysis of this growing discontent an important concern of his office. He has prepared a special report for the president on blue-collar disenchantment, and has addressed major organizations such as the American Management Association on the theme. Rosow says, "Millions of workers . . . are getting increasingly frustrated. . . . their work life is unsatisfactory but they see no way of breaking out . . . their total life pattern is discouraging." He finds that promotion opportunities are "restricted by mobility patterns within firms; lack of information about better jobs in other firms. . . ." Rosow cites a University of Michigan Survey Research Center study showing that American workers generally expect that working entitles them to more than a paycheck, and that "job challenge or 'interesting work' was rated by workers as *the single most important* aspect of job satisfaction." Repetitive tasks that restrict personal freedom and limit decision-making are at the root of much of the feelings of alienation, he says. Fairness of promotions, and the promotion opportunities themselves, have a major impact on the workers' attitudes, he continues. And he quotes findings published in *Fortune* magazine as evidence of the fact that "younger workers today, much more than in past generations, expect to participate in the decision-making processes in their job-world, and may turn dissatisfaction with working conditions into poor job performance and job attendance."

There is abundant other evidence that the labor viewpoint expressed by the AFL-CIO's Pollara is, at the very least, open to question. A survey recently completed by Neal Q. Herrick, federal executive fellow with the W. E. Upjohn Institute for Employment Research, is particularly convincing. Herrick questioned management officials, labor union leaders, and groups of white-collar and blue-collar workers. He found that management thinks workers' opportunities to grow and achieve on the job need improvement as much or more than their pay, and that "the workers rank interesting and satisfying work over pay—indeed, blue-collar workers rank pay a poor last on their list of needed improvements." Union officials, however, were "singularly unimpressed" with the need to improve job content, "at least when they stacked it up against the need to improve the economic aspects of the work situation." In view of the opinions expressed both by management and workers about the need for job improvements, Herrick questions whether "unions might give some thought to whether or not they are taking the right issues to the bargaining table." It has been mentioned earlier that this is just what the younger labor leaders are likely to do as they begin to take over from the older generation.

Desirable and desired though they may be, bringing about job improvements is never easy, and the path is rarely without obstacles, both foreseeable and unforeseen. Dr. Michael Beer of the Corning Glass Works has made useful comments about several of the problems that have to be surmounted. If there is not considerable trust between workers and management, he says, job enrichment will not be accepted readily. Where trust is lacking, it has to be nurtured. Beer says it is necessary, at the very least, to "make it clear that employe participation in the change will be helpful in increasing understanding and trust." Another issue that can become thorny is pay. If employe responsibility is increased, Beer says, the job must be reevaluated and the pay scale raised where warranted. This can bring up the question of where the values lie for the organization, Beer notes, but he believes that job enrichments will result in gains for the organization, not only in volume produced but in the flexibility of the employe and his increased contribution of ideas and suggestions.

Job enrichment also affects the supervisors' jobs, Beer says. They must be trained to adopt new roles as teachers and trainers of their subordinates, as the jobs they supervise become more complex. Training in their new roles is necessary, too, to avoid their feeling diminished as more of their responsibilities are delegated. Beer cautions against forcing job enrichment on an entire group of workers, and suggests instead that it be approached on an individual basis. Otherwise, he says, added responsibilities may be forced on those who do not want them.

Oddly enough, if job enrichment is carried out successfully, it results in what Beer calls "a whole new set of problems for the manager," but these, he says, will "hopefully be high-class problems of managing the motivated employe. Workers who have tasted a sense of achievement will demand more, putting a strain on the organization to meet these new and rising expectations."

Beer says that a basic restructuring of roles in the organization is inherent in the concept of job enrichment. "Greater responsibility is thrust on lower levels, and therefore greater trust in individuals is required by those at higher levels." This means a certain dispersal or diffusion of authority, but at the same time more widespread involvement and commitment. "It should be clear to anyone embarking on job enrichment that the value to the organization does not always lie in increased production volume. The benefits may be in more subtle areas such as greater employe flexibility, increased quality, and more innovation. With the increased pace of change in the world of work, these will become more and more important considerations in the future."

It must be evident from everything that has gone before that injecting job enrichment into an organization and making it work is not easy. But the need to try is so imperative, the pressures demanding it are so great, and the results so rewarding that the risks are dwarfed by the potential advantages. From management's view, the benefits include better quality products, a richer flow of production-increasing and cost-cutting ideas, fewer personnel disagreements and grievances, fewer discipline and absentee problems, and a pleasanter working atmosphere. From the viewpoint of the workers, it can mean satisfaction with one's work and a degree of pride in it, improved morale and a feeling of accomplishment, and in a broader sense, a better and far more rewarding existence. Looking at the situation from the broad perspective of society's needs and concerns, better jobs can mean a better and richer life for the country, greater prosperity as productivity improves and the nation's ability to compete economically is enhanced, and a stronger feeling of family between different groups in the country. One of the serious problems facing the United States is the proliferation of divisions, in every direction and at every level in the country. Politically, the right excoriates the left. Socially, the privileged are divided from those less privileged. Economically, the poor resent the rich, and with welfare causing the intense arguments it does, the rich seem to resent the poor just as cordially. Within families, young people oppose their elders. There are divisions between city dwellers and non-city dwellers. There is the vice-president against liberals, and reporters. There are racial divisions. Now, to complete the list of schisms, we have women squaring off against men. This frightening variety of divisions presents a host of dangers for a society as totally interdependent as ours, where a small number of angry people can tie up a city's utilities or a country's communications by technological means available to practically everyone. In a closely linked structure such as this, already under high tension, we simply cannot afford to have workers hate their bosses or hate their jobs, or managers hate their employes. It would be a great and grave danger to the nation.

Jean-François Revel writes in *Without Marx or Jesus: the New American Revolution Has Begun,* a passage peculiarly relevant to the topic of changes in work. The passage relates to the new demands for freedom on the part of younger people, including younger workers, in America. "Today in America . . . a new revolution is rising. It is the revolution of our time. It is the only revolution that involves radical, moral, and practical opposition to the spirit of nationalism. It is the only revolution that, to that opposition, joins culture, economic and technological power, and a total affirmation of liberty for all in place of archaic prohibitions. It, therefore, offers the only possible escape for mankind today: the acceptance of technological civilization as a means and not as an end, and—since we cannot be saved either by the destruction of the civilization or by its continuation —the development of the ability to reshape that civilization without annihilating it."

This passage speaks on many levels and of many things, but it can be taken as an eloquent expression of the need to give men more freedom in every aspect of their lives, including their work, and to avoid their being chained by technology.

One of America's great scientific and industrial geniuses, Dr. Edwin H. Land, of the Polaroid Corporation, has seen the need to improve jobs for years, and the progress he has made in doing so has contributed importantly to the extraordinary success of his company. The handbook given employes at Polaroid has on its first page a statement by Dr. Land entitled "The Purpose of Our Company." It says: "We have two basic aims here at Polaroid." One is defined as the manufacture of useful, high-quality products. "The other," the statement continues, "is to give everyone working for Polaroid personal opportunity within the Company for full exercise of his talents; to express his opinions, to share in the progress of the Company as far as his capacities permit, to earn enough money so that the need for earning more will not always be the first thing on his mind—opportunity, in short, to make his work here a fully rewarding, important part of his life."

This extraordinarily prescient and profound statement, publicly proclaimed twenty-seven years ago as one of the twin pillars on which a great American business has been built, could and should serve as a model for every company that wants to help itself and help its workers. It illustrates that the long-range goal of efforts to improve jobs and the climate in which they are performed, on a higher plane than merely smoothing operations and increasing profits, is that of enabling a company to serve the deepest needs of the human beings working for it, and of the society in which it exists. In an era of increasing doubt about the validity of the usual corporate goals—doubt that has sharply reduced the desire of young people to enter business—making jobs better and more responsive to men's wants and ambitions becomes social service of a high order. Inventor-philosopher-executive Edwin Land expresses the aim well. "It is a wonderful phenomenon," he says, "to see people serving a cause and working together to share a task. It is only through a unifying purpose that interpersonal aggressiveness and destructiveness can be subordinated."

Helping people to work together rather than in competition, and making jobs more personally rewarding, are the kind of objectives, and tactics, that will attract idealistic younger workers. Encouraging participation and allowing them a sense of controlling their own destinies, rather than requiring rote learning and ritual obedience, these are approaches that without question will benefit companies questing in the competition for the best manpower and womanpower available. Thus job enrichment can bring not only present profit, but it can also enhance the likelihood of constructive growth for the corporation, improve the lives of all those associated with it, and in this way signally serve the society in which we all function.

# INDEX

## A

# B

# D

# E

# *I*

Leadership
    demand for intelligent, 19
    progressive, of American corporations, 20
    Uttermahlen's comments about, 19
    white-collar, 82
Lehrer, Tom, 7
Levi Strauss and Co., 151, 160
Levinson, Harry, 150
*Life* magazine, 19
Likert, Rensis, Dr., 62, 94, 165, 170, 171
Lordstown, Ohio, 113
Lovell, Malcolm J., Jr., 49

# M

Management
    closeness to, dwindling, 33
    courses, 127
    job shifts among junior, 82
    junior, antagonisms of, 42
    -labor relationships, 179-180
Management Achievement Program, 146
MAP, 147
Marine Midland Bank, 153
Maslow, Abraham H., 90, 111
Massachusetts Institute of Technology, 52
MBA Enterprises, Inc., 41
Mechanical robots, 114
Mechanization, 125
Medical care, assistance of, to every individual, 3
Memorex, 154
Menninger Foundation, 150
Meylan, Lenz, 131